D1859537

AN INTERPRETATION OF INDIA'S RELIGIOUS HISTORY

AN INTERPRETATION OF INDIA'S RELIGIOUS HISTORY

ROBERT A. HUME, D. D.

GYAN

Published by

Gyan Publishing House
5, Ansari Road
Daryaganj, New Delhi-110002
Phone: 011-47034999, 9811692060
E-mail: books@gyanbooks.com

Distribution Network
gyanbooks.com
India, USA, Canada, UK, Australia, France

ISBN: 978-81-212-9384-6 (PB)
First Published, 1911

2nd Impression 2023

Printed at: Gyan Press, Delhi.

AN INTERPRETATION OF INDIA'S RELIGIOUS HISTORY

AUTHOR: ROBERT A. HUME

AN INTERPRETATION OF INDIA'S RELIGIOUS HISTORY

AN INTERPRETATION OF INDIA'S RELIGIOUS HISTORY

By

ROBERT A. HUME, D.D.

WITH INTRODUCTION BY

HENRY CHURCHILL KING, D.D., LL.D.

President of Oberlin College

NEW YORK CHICAGO TORONTO

Fleming H. Revell Company

LONDON AND EDINBURGH

INTRODUCTION

IT seems almost an impertinence for one without an experience in India like Dr. Hume's to attempt even a brief introduction to these illuminating lectures on the religious history of India. Dr. Hume needs no outsider's commendation or correction; for he writes out of the treasures of long residence and devoted service in India, of painstaking study of its life and thought, and of sympathetic and reverent appreciation of its religious development.

But one may well express his gratitude for the precise nature of the aim and spirit of these lectures, and for the detailed illustrations in which aim and spirit are indicated. For the distinguishing characteristic of the lectures is, that they are in earnest with Christ's conception of God as Father of all men, and strive to look at the complex religious phenomena of India in that light. Dr. Hume sees clearly, that, for the Christian man, who really believes that God is Father, the great difficulty to-day is not to account for the good in the non-Christian religions; but as he says, "the more perplexing problem is how to account for arrest and degeneracy in religion and society." In the light of God's Fatherhood, the Christian does not grant reluctantly any evidences of the working of the Spirit of God among all peoples, but rejoices in them; he needs such evidences to keep his faith in Christ's conception of God. And, he needs also to understand just how degeneracy crept in; and he will see this most clearly in comparisons with religious phenomena with which he is more familiar. Such a Christian, therefore, will be grateful for the detailed way in which Dr. Hume helps him to see the parallels between the religious development of India and that of the West, both in its advances, and in its losses. There is no attempt to disguise the facts on either side; there is clear criticism, as well as warm appreciation, but in both cases the insight is the insight of faith and love—of faith in the Fatherhood of God, and love for his Indian "brothers," as he truly feels them to be.

Dr. Hume naturally assumes that we may not take it for granted that Western interpretations have exhausted the meaning of Christ for men, but that we may, rather, rationally expect a valuable supplement to Western interpretations from the honest reaction of the Indian mind on the great Christian facts.

Dr. Hume does not attempt an elaborate scientific essay in comparative religion, but the brevity and seeming simplicity of the lectures may easily obscure for one the large amount of thoughtful observation and study packed into them. The more earnestly one has himself tried to think through the complex and puzzling phenomena of the religious life in India, the more likely is he to appreciate what Dr. Hume has here accomplished.

HENRY CHURCHILL KING.

OBERLIN COLLEGE.

CONTENTS

I

AN INTERPRETIVE OUTLINE OF INDIA'S EARLIER RELIGIOUS HISTORY

IN a religious history of the world an account of the religious thought and life of India would form one of the most important sections, because it would be the theme of a large part of the entire life of a most religious people, extending over a long period. Libraries have been written on the subject without covering it. One reason is that obscurity veils much of the story. Most of the life of ancient generations of every people has naturally passed into oblivion. Fortunately India's religious memorials, enshrined in her literature, give a part of her religious experience. But ancient books give mainly the religious conceptions of the thinkers. Yet the power of any religion is more in what it makes the masses do than in what it leads either the classes or the masses to profess to believe. Another reason why scholars have not covered the whole story of India's religious history is the variety and complexity of the thought and life of that multitudinous people.

Nevertheless, there are some fairly well known characteristics of that history. Those who desire the utmost spiritual development of that country, and who believe that the Christ can give this development, need an interpretation of how its varying religious beliefs and practices arose and mingled with and modified one another; how they grew, suffered arrest of development and degeneration; how efforts at reform sometimes succeeded and sometimes failed; what the large outcome of these movements has been; what is the present state of thought and life in that land; and what appears to be the outlook for the future. Such an effort in brief compass must unavoidably be quite general, and doubtless will be imperfect. The justification for an attempt lies in the need of such an interpretation, and in the experience of the writer, who was born in Bombay, who has spent thirty-six years of adult missionary service in western India, and who has deep love and high hope for his native land.

The assumption underlying this attempt is that God has been ever seeking His Indian children; that He has never left Himself without witness among them; that with many limitations and errors the people of India have diligently sought after God in eager desire that, haply they might find Him, though He has never been far from them; that He mercifully bore with those times of limitation and ignorance; that, as to earlier generations of Israel God spoke through Hebrew prophets by divers portions and in divers manners, so to previous generations of Indians God spoke more or less distinctly by Indian thinkers and saints; but that now He is speaking to His children by His Son, the Lord Jesus Christ, who is the effulgence of His glory and His very image. This assumption is coupled with the ardent desire and expectation that the gifted Indian children of the Father of all spirits will, under the guidance of the universal Spirit, find and accept in the Lord Jesus Christ the fulfiller of their long aspiration and search, and that, so finding and accepting Him, they will be inspired by the divine Spirit marvellously to interpret Him to their brethren throughout the world.

The best illustration of the statement that man is "incurably religious" is found in the Hindu people. "Religion" influences their thought and conduct from before birth until after death. What made the Hindu such? God. Have we not all one Father? Is He the God of the Christians only? Is He not the God of the Hindus also? Yea, of the Hindus also. The Christian must more fully and more gladly accept Christ's assumption and teaching of the Heavenly Father's impartial blessing on all His children.

Devout science scrutinizes every potentiality in the physical and mental world as a thought and purpose of God, awaiting liberation and larger utility. Devout spiritual science must be equally open-eyed and hopeful in its scrutiny of every potentiality in the spiritual world. More and more it *is* thus alert. Comparative religion and psychology are showing that the fundamental elements of religion are found everywhere.

Psychology and sociology are coming to recognize a larger and larger element of esthetic instincts and developments in children and in primitive peoples. Hence we are placing a higher valuation on the religious capacity and religious attainments of non-Christian peoples, and therefore are taking a more respectful and sympathetic attitude n thinking how the more advanced peoples can, and should, bear themselves in dealing with backward communities. If this is the correct attitude for those who study the languages and social institutions of less advanced peoples, how much more should the spirit of ppreciation and respect characterize and animate those who thoroughly believe in God and who, from profound hope in Him, seek o be helpful religiously to all peoples.

> "Thrice blessed is he to whom is given the
> instinct that can tell
> That God is in the field when He is
> most invisible."

One fundamental reason why earnest Christians have not yet adequately recognized

God's influence in the best elements of the religious habits and thoughts of non-Christians is the failure to distinguish carefully, continuously, and gladly between a spiritual value and its outward expression in language and rite. It is not children alone who find it hard to distinguish between the thing and its name. The Lord Jesus Christ was misunderstood, criticised, hated, and put to death by religious zealots because He did distinguish between the name and the thing in religion. He cared nothing for the name, but cared everything for the genuine thing in religion. He was infinitely pained by the formality and hypocrisy which had no reality of spiritual experience, while assuming that it was the possessor and divinely appointed guardian of the truth, because it used religious terms which were hallowed from a period when those terms expressed an experience which afterwards was lost in traditionalism and formality.

It is now time for Missions to take advantage of the movement against traditionalism in the West by applying similar tests to ascertain what fundamental spiritual value there may be in thought and life among non-Christian peoples, despite immense degeneracy in the expressions of that thought and life. By such service Missions may give reflex help to the Western movement against traditionalism, which seeks for spiritual reality, and which is often misunderstood and opposed, as was the Lord Jesus Christ misunderstood and opposed, by many at home who deem themselves the guardians of truth.

If we believe that God has always been the chief actor, even in the religions of non-Christians, then why has not the Hindu religion been more satisfactory than the Christian believes it to have been? Because the Hindu has his full share of the limitations and sins of humanity. Some of these limitations and sins are great difficulty in seeing things in proper proportions, that is, the common tendency to take a part for the whole; when disillusioned by the excess and unsatisfactoriness of one-half of the truth, the habit of going to the other extreme, for example now to consider the outside the whole of a thing, and anon to think its whole to be the inside; pride of the intellect; unworthy contentment with lower things instead of eagerness for the best; disregard of brother men, and imagining that there is a way of life with God apart from love to His human children; and finally no experience of God's supreme revelation in the Lord Jesus Christ until recently. These are the reasons which account for the unsatisfactoriness of Hindu religious thought and life. The man who finds in the Lord Jesus Christ a balance, a universality, a dynamic satisfying and inspiring to intellect, heart, and will, who makes Him the Lord of his life, and who therefore draws from his Master character like His, simply must, from very joy and gratitude, desire and strive to impart to brother men everywhere what he has himself received and what that Lord wishes to impart through him to others. In a word, the Lord Jesus Christ being the completest, the balanced, revelation of God and the loving, suffering Son of Man, He is the moral magnet and the spiritual dynamic of the world.

Nor is the Christian adequately qualified

to interpret God's work in the religious thought and life of the world, if he does not always couple with the spiritual dynamic of the Christ the universal, all-powerful, ceaseless activity of the Holy Spirit of God. Was not the Holy Spirit at work for the Hebrew people before the time of the Christ? Unquestionably. What the Christ did was to free men's minds and to assure man that the divine Pedagogue is a real, eternal, universal, ever active guide for all men, though now having in the character, teachings, life, and sufferings of the Christ a supremer instrument for His work than the world had previously known. Was that universal, divine Pedagogue doing nothing for Hindus till after the departure of the Christ? They who seem to think so would deny the divinity of the Holy Spirit. Being divine and universal, of course He was doing all that in that stage of every nation's history He could do.

The thoughtful man who thus believes in the perpetual and beneficent activity of the Holy Spirit can not only affirm, but truly and thankfully believe, that in the entire history of mankind there is one far-off divine event to which the whole creation moves, that there is a divine activity and purpose in every part of the story of the world. God has never failed steadily to adhere to His one purpose. The sad, pathetic element in the world's religious history is man's misapprehension, or partial apprehension, or rejection of God's fatherly effort for him.

> "Nothing walks with aimless feet;
> Not one life shall be destroyed,
> Or cast as rubbish to the void,
> When God hath made the pile complete."

The vision of the Christ ought also to accomplish two more important effects on the spirit of such a man. One effect should be a sense of humility for the limitations and errors of himself and of others who bear the Christian name. The other effect should be encouragement at finding in brother men who have not previously enjoyed a knowledge of the Christ some preparation for Him, coupled with humble recognition of the fact that, to broaden and quicken the thought and life of himself and other Christians, these need from some non-Christians some truths which those have received. Too often the Christian enthusiast has not realized that a humble readiness to learn is a Christian virtue needed to qualify him for his task as well as zeal to impart what he has already received. As in other spheres, so in religion the principle holds,—give and it shall be given unto you; good measure, pressed down, shaken together, running over shall they give into your bosom.

No man and no community is a self-centred unit. All men and all religions are bound into an organic whole. The principle of instrumentality, of mediation, is God's method. The Bible is one long illustration of man's mistaken desire to be a separate unit, dependent on his own thoughts and plans. But God's thoughts have ever been higher than men's thoughts, and God's ways than men's ways. Through His teaching to every human child God has planned to do something for His other children. Neither Hindu, nor Persian, nor Egyptian, nor Greek, nor Hebrew, nor the average Christian has *known* all that God planned to do through him by what He did for him. Even to the most clear-sighted of the prophets and poets of all nations have been given inspirations and ideals beyond and above their ken. Not only to the great Persian could God say, "Cyrus, my anointed; I have surnamed thee, thou hast not known Me. I will gird thee, though thou hast not known Me; that at last they may know from the rising of the sun and from the west that there is none beside Me. I am the Lord." The spiritual interpreter of the past must see and confess that many another religious leader in many lands has been the unconscious, but anointed, instrument of God to help the world sooner or later to the one Christlike God, the Father of the spirits of all men. When the Lord Jesus says, "I am the way, the truth, and the life; no man cometh unto the Father but by Me," He means that He is and shows the way of God *to* men, even before He is, and shows, men's way to God. And by revealing God as the Father He teaches that God is ready not only for the future to do His utmost for every human child, but also that in the past He has done His workable best for all men.

Before beginning a large interpretation of India's religious history, it seemed desirable thus briefly to state the assumptions and principles on which the attempt is made, and also to give some forecast of the conclusion which is being drawn. But in order to attempt such interpretation it is necessary first to give at least an outline of that history. The present lecture will attempt an interpretive outline of the earlier history of India up to the decline of the Buddhist movement. The next lecture will give an outline of India's later religious history from the rise of modern Hinduism to its recent contact with the West. The third lecture will attempt an analysis of the most significant characteristics of dominant Hinduism. The subsequent lecture will be a characterization of the greatness and the weakness of Hinduism. The final lecture will seek to show how India's religious history has prepared her to receive and to interpret the Christ, and how the Christ has power to meet that preparation.

I briefly forecast what in my judgment will be the conclusions reached in these lectures.

As we run through an outline of India's history, in my judgment four words will correctly epitomize the characteristics of that history:—progress, arrest, degeneracy, and reform—all four repeated over and over again through millenniums. During that long period India's religious gamut runs from fetishism through animism, polytheism, dualism, pantheism, theism to incipient monotheism, with many a discord and false note, yet, on the whole, rising higher. India's religious history is full of illustrations of the age-long struggle of the spirit against the flesh and of the flesh against the spirit, with victory now for one and now for the other. It is a panorama of the struggle which occurs in every religion between the letter and the spirit, between metaphysics and life, between a mechanical and a spiritual view of religion. God's attitude toward man must always have been the same before and since the Christ. Christ only revealed, and the Holy Spirit taking the things of Christ is more and more revealing, what God's eternal attitude is. Where the Christ has revealed God's real attitude toward His human children, men have begun to understand that the fundamental relation between God and His children is one in which He is the first and chief agent, suffering because His children are ignorant of and estranged from Him, that He is ever exerting His divine power in seeking them in order to bring them into harmonious filial life, and therefore that their religious thinking and acting are their response to His call, however feeble and mistaken that response may be.

While India's religious history is encouraging because it shows that, despite limitations, errors, and sin, the Hindu has made a response to the divine voice, it is depressing because the Hindu has failed to understand the heart of religion—that what man needs is not so much to seek after God as to accept the God who is seeking him. God is the great Reality in actual relation to every soul. The age-long, fundamental errors of Hindu theology have been that the universe and world are unreal, that escape from its delusive unreality is secured by the intellectual belief that Reality is only a metaphysical conception, and that this intellectual belief is to be gained by whittling away every vital experience and imagining that the thing—in itself—without relations is the great reality.

A correct review of India's religious history should also reveal the working of the principles of genetic psychology. These principles have been at work among Hindus as much as among any other peoples. By their fruits ye shall know them is a biological law in every department. No one who well knows the Hindu will fail to recognize a vivid illustration of pathetic arrest in the Indian in many, perhaps in all, departments of his marvellous make-up. One of the acutest interpreters of India's history, Meredith Townsend, speaks thus: "Some strange fiat of arrest has condemned the brown men and the yellow men to eternal reproduction of old ideas. They have treated the earth as if they feared it. . . . From end to end of Asia great stores of iron or platinum or tin, of copper, silver, or gold, lie untouched waiting for the touch of the European spoiler. . . . If the energy in digging which once was in Asia had continued, even the riches of Asia would by this time have been exhausted." This arrest of development in practical matters has been accompanied by arrest in spiritual development also. And arrest is ordinarily the prelude to degeneracy. No proverb or principle is more universally accepted by the Hindu than that in many respects Hinduism is now in a degenerate stage; that there have been in Hinduism four ages, the *Satya, Treta, Dvapar,* and *Kali Yugas,* which might be termed the golden, silver, iron, and earthen or evil ages, in the latter of which Hinduism now finds itself. Any institution or organism has suffered arrest and is suffering degeneracy when its golden age is in the past. Also, in India there has been, and is, a widespread belief that the coming better age will be ushered in by a Kalki Avatar, i.e. a suffering, yet victorious, incarnation. It is for the Christian to show that the Christ will fulfill that anticipation, will stop the arrest and degeneracy, and will develop a marvellous spiritual age, partly at least, through the sympathetic, self-denying, respectful, fraternal aid of brother Christians who are full of the Christ-like spirit.

Also the history of Hinduism distinctly shows the working of both the upward and downward trend apparent in the principles of genetic psychology: superstition develops into a simple, naïve, cheerful relation to gods, into greater intellectual thought, into a recognition of laws, into legalism, into a sense of disobedience to law, into a sense of the need of grace and experience of grace, into declines and reforms, followed by new declines and new uplifts repeated over and over again, till now the Christ is already giving to India a life and a power which are prophetic of greater development to come. In the parable of the wheat and tares, to Christ's disciples, the mystery lay not in the growth of the wheat, but of the tares. In the history of non-Christian religions, to many Christians, the mystery has been in the growth of the wheat, not of the tares, which were easily supposed to be all, or nearly all, the crop in those religions, and which were considered due to the evil one. Now that wheat also is seen to be growing in the field of non-Christian faiths, to some Christians the mystery seems to be to whom the wheat is to be credited. They have not been accustomed to look for wheat in the non-Christian religions, and, if wheat were found, they could hardly credit it to God. To-day the more perplexing problem is how to account for arrest and degeneracy in religion and in society. But hardly any warning is more solemn and suggestive to those who call themselves Christians and yet are self-centred and self-satisfied than one from history which is "full of saddening examples of how the most hopeful movements have come to an evil end because those in charge of them have treated their work, and themselves, as the centre of the universe, instead of as a mere planet revolving round the central orb of the divine will." The theology of some men and races has remained Ptolemaic, though their astronomy was Copernican.

With this introductory statement of assumptions and principles underlying this attempt, I now turn to a brief interpretive outline of the religious history of India. Five thousand years ago the religion of the dark-skinned peoples of Kolarian or Dravidian races who inhabited Hindustan was one in which the worship of serpents, trees, the phallus, and similar objects was common. Magic and witchcraft to avoid evils which men feared were the common elements of their belief and practice. Cunning men were set apart for the purpose, and performed the magical rites of the religion of those aborigines. Though it was a superstitious religion of degrading practices, administered by men who were ignorant and often cruel, yet it was a response to the god whom they worshipped, mainly because they feared him. The religion of most of the people of India has advanced beyond this low phase. Yet to this day millions of the descendants of those aborigines largely follow that superstitious system, and it has also corrupted and modified the religion of the Aryans, who brought a higher religion into the land.

Somewhere in the interval of from three thousand to twelve hundred years before the Christian era there came to India, from the northwest, successive immigrations of peoples of a race commonly called Aryans. The characteristics of the religion of these new-comers can be well determined from the Rig Veda, a collection of 1018 hymns in ten books. Because these hymns, covering a period of from seven hundred to one thousand years, differ among themselves and are not chronologically arranged, one cannot give a positive opinion about the exact chronological development of the religious thought and life of those Aryan settlers through so long a period as from seven to ten centuries. But the emotions and reflections of a quick-witted people could not remain unchanged through such a long period. The Rig Veda was followed by three other collections of hymns called the Sama, Yajur, and Atharva Vedas which are full of directions for religious practices. In general scholars can give an approximately correct estimate as to which hymns are earliest, which of an intermediate period, and which were the latest. In addition to the contents of the hymns, the main clue comes from the analogy of religious evolution elsewhere, and from the later history of Indian thought. The religion of the Aryans was at first one of appreciation of the brighter aspects of external nature, partly personified as gods, yet somewhat influenced by intimations of an unseen world. Their hymns were chants sung in the open air at sunrise, noonday, and sunset, but especially at sunrise around a simple family altar, without temples and without priests. They prayed for such blessings as good crops, the birth of children, success in war, etc., much as children nowadays pray for material blessings. The dawn and the sun naturally were prominent, and as the expellers of darkness were adored as divine. In all its varied aspects and activities the sun is the most striking and forceful object in nature. The nineteenth psalm in the Biblical book of Psalms illustrates how the sun affected a Hebrew poet who said that "Nothing is hid from the heat thereof." It is not strange that the simple Aryans adored and worshipped the sun under various names, such as Mitra, meaning "a friend," or Vishnu, representing the pervading activity of the sun. One hymn of the Rig Vedas says, "O Sun, with the light with which thou overcomest darkness, and rousest the whole world in splendour, with that light drive away from us all weakness, all negligence, all illness and sleeplessness." Another hymn says, "Seeing the light rise higher and higher above the darkness, we come to the highest light, to Surya [the sun], the god among the gods." The low invisible wind which whispered in men's ears easily suggested a spirit. In the Bible and in the religions of Rome and Greece the name of the Spirit is the word for wind. This earlier Aryan religion clearly shows how a belief in many gods arose. The manifold manifestations of power in Nature were personified, and each personified manifestation received a name and each *nomen* easily became a *numen*. Among unsophisticated men of little logical thought personification of a natural object was due to a spiritually vitalized impression or experience leading to a spiritualized expression. This was the origin of Aryan polytheism. God touched the life of the primitive Aryan with manifold blessing, and the simple man's heart responded with a divine name for each manifestation. The cardinal features of this early Aryan religion were direct access to the gods, direct benefits in answer to prayers and offerings, and consequent fervency of prayer and meditation, and lavishness of praise and sacrifice which secured the desired blessings. This was spiritual progress from the superstition and magical religion of the aborigines.

In that earliest Vedic religion sacrifices were a prominent feature, but they were not propitiatory offerings to appease an offended deity. They were feasts to which the gods were invited as guests. The wood of the sacrificial altar was ignited by the householder, himself striking together two pieces of wood, and then this fire (Agni) was personified and adored as divine because it seemed a blending of something which man could not do co-operating with man in consuming the offering. Here the religion of the Hindu met arrest, which was soon followed by degeneracy.

The next development of the Aryan religion was a downward one when the letter choked the spirit. In the Yajur and the Atharva Vedas sacrifice has become the principal thing in religion. The sacrifice is now supposed to appease the god and to influence him to do what the worshipper wished. There were sacrifices of all sorts of animals, including the horse and the cow, and occasionally even human sacrifices. When such importance was ascribed to sacrifice the next downward step was that the sacrifice itself had power to compel the gods, or to have power in itself independently of God. And when the sacrifice was made both elaborate and supreme, the next easy downward step was to make the priest the supreme element in religion because only he could properly conduct an elaborate and important service. When has not the supposition that God must be appeased by a sacrifice, and the consequent elevating of the sacredness and power of the official who performs the sacrifice, led to a sacerdotal and mechanical view of religion? This was a victory of the flesh over the spirit.

This development led to another downward step which is illustrated in the last of the Vedas, the Atharva Veda, namely the necessity and power of charms both for blessing and cursing. Whereas the early type of the Aryan religion was a victory over the degrading religion of the aborigines, now the characteristics of the latter seem to have become the chief elements of even the Aryan religion. In the later Vedic period the Atharva Veda became the most influential religious book of the Hindus, and is called " a picture of the lower life of ancient India. It exhibits the ordinary Hindu, not only in the aspect of a devout and virtuous worshipper of the gods and the performer of pious practices, but also as demon-plagued, fear-ridden, hateful, lustful, and addicted to sorcery." It was one of the frequent and sad victories of the flesh over the spirit of which India's religious history is full.

On the other hand, the Vedas also show one gratifying and upward movement in religion, which was the high-water mark of the earlier religious history of India, viz.: the development of an incipient monotheism. The one early Vedic deity who had a distinctly moral character was Varuna, who in name and in sphere, like the Greek *ouranos,* originally indicated the firmament. In his case the grandeur of the physical firmament became united with moral grandeur, and Vedic poets ascribed to Varuna activities similar to those which Hebrew poets ascribed to Jehovah. If a similar result in the history of Israel is to be ascribed to the Spirit of God, then this upward movement in India also deserves to be similarly credited to God. In one hymn it is said of Varuna, "Wise and mighty are the works of him who stemmed asunder the firmaments. He lifted on high the bright and glorious heaven; he stretched out apart the starry sky and the earth." In another hymn it is said that Varuna had opened a path for the sun; he knows the track of the bird through the air, and of the ships across the seas, and there is nothing hid from his sight. He possesses universal sovereignty and is the lord of nature and of men. His thousand spies go forth throughout the world and bring back reports of what men are doing. More than any other Vedic deity Varuna is a moral sovereign, who awakens in men a sense of sin. One hymn of the Atharva Veda, which scholars consider an early hymn, says, "The great guardian among the gods sees as if from anear. . . . If two sit together and steal, King Varuna is there as the third, and knows it. . . . Whoso should flee beyond the heavens far away would not yet be free from King Varuna. . . . From the sky his spies come hither; with a thousand eyes they do watch over the earth. What is between the two firmaments and what beyond, all this doth King Varuna behold. Numbered of him are the winkings of men's eyes." In a hymn of the Rig Veda the singer conceives of himself as forsaken by Varuna on account of sin, and so asks, "What hath become of those our ancient friendships when without enmity we walked together? . . . O Varuna, if thy true ally hath sinned against thee, still he is the friend thou lovedst." Varuna's moral dignity rises still higher because he is thought to be a god to note, to forgive, and to put away sin. Professor Macdonnell, of Oxford, says that, "There is in fact no hymn to Varuna in which the prayer for forgiveness does not occur, as in the hymns to the other deities the prayer for worldly goods." The following are examples of such addresses to this most ethical of Vedic gods: "Far from us, far away drive thou destruction. Put from us even the sin which we have committed." Other hymns say that Varuna "places his fetters upon the sinner; his is the power to bind and the power also to release, and he forgives sin even unto the second generation."

Probably the most marked recognition of Varuna as a god of moral sovereignty is his special connection with the moral order which is called *ṛta* in Vedic literature. A word of the same origin and meaning occurs in the Iranian religion. From this we know that the thought of a cosmic order was with the Aryan from very early times. But in most of the Vedic religion so moral a conception was vague and rare. The objects in the visible world and the regularly recurring events of nature were assumed to be regulated by the cosmic order or *ṛta*. But only to a limited extent was this cosmic order thought of as also a moral order of righteousness, save in connection with the god Varuna. Yet this highest conception of Varuna as a righteous deity can only be called an incipient monotheism, since Varuna was always only one of many gods, though in the earlier Vedic religion we see more of henotheism than polytheism, i.e. the singer considered the god whom he named as practically the one all-powerful god. The many gods were largely many names of one god, much as monotheists now apply many epithets to the only God whom they acknowledge.

In addition to recognizing Varuna as a personal and righteous god, some Vedic worshippers gave a spiritual turn to their religion by a somewhat vivid conception of a personal relation between the worshipper and god through faith. In the earlier Vedic times the word for faith (*shrāddha*) somewhat expressed reverential trust as well as intellectual belief. It expressed both intellectual conviction concerning the existence and power of the gods and also reverence toward them. It implied a sense both of reality and of trust. Thus in one place it is said: "The lord of creatures [Prajāpati] having beheld two qualities, separated truth and lie from one another. He put unfaith into lie; faith he placed into truth." But as in other religions, so in this early simple religion, the letter began to kill the spirit, and the word faith, which should be principally an expression for an attitude of the heart, became the name for an act of the intellect alone, or acquiescence in a prevalent theory or doctrine; and faith became identified with knowledge. Then, as in other religions, a still lower value was given to faith by the assumption that the intellectual act called faith had religious power of itself. Not so the New Testament writer who said, "The devils believe and tremble." Then the vivid imagination and personifying habit of the Hindus semi-personified such faith and adored it as a goddess. Thus in one place it is said:

> "Through Faith the gods obtain their divine quality;
> Faith, the goddess, is the foundation of the world.
> Faith do we revere without oblations;
> May she create for us an immortal world."

And again:

> "Faith dwells in the gods,
> Faith dwells upon this world,

Faith the mother of wishes—
With oblations do we prosper her."

Such a conception of the relation of a worshipper with a deity was a downward movement, for it led men to consider religion as mainly the intellectual conception of a certain doctrine, or else the performance of prescribed acts, in order to secure desired material blessings. Then the next step was the assumption that the way to get the desired blessings lay through giving abundant gifts to the priest, to influence him to perform the prescribed rites. In turn this influenced the priests mostly to desire in their religious thought and life large gifts for performing the rites. In what religion has not sacramentarianism been a cause and an indication of spiritual decay? And when has it not been swiftly followed by the next downward step, namely, sacerdotalism, which degraded the worshipper, and still more the mechanical priest?

After the flesh had thus debased Indian religion, under the influence of the divine Spirit the pious Hindu revolted from such a mechanical system and the next development of the Vedic religion was an entire swing of the pendulum from nature worship, polytheism, and ceremonialism to the final type of Vedic religion, viz.: philosophical speculation. Just when, where, and how this way of thinking began is uncertain. There are traces of it in the earliest Vedic hymns. Thoughtful men began to ask the whence and how, and whither of the universe and of themselves. Any simple man who stops to think about the mysterious changes which are constantly occurring, cannot help sometimes wondering what the explanation of such matters is. And later, when sacrificial ceremonies were conducted on a large scale, men could not but marvel at the alleged mystic power of these rites, and question why extreme importance was attached to performing them with mechanical exactness. Some Indian philosophical books give examples of the way in which kings and priests propounded an answer to questions connected with the performance of great sacrifices. Scholars say that such religious riddles are probably unknown in any religion except that of India. The word for speculative discussion is *brahmavidya,* i.e. speculation about Brahma, or the ultimate reality. The following is an example of such a discussion at a horse sacrifice (*ashvamedha*). One priest asks: "Who, verily, moveth quite alone; who, verily, is born again and again; what, forsooth, is the remedy for cold; and what is the greatest pile?" Another priest answers: "The sun moveth quite alone; the moon is born again and again; fire is the remedy for cold; the earth is the greatest pile." Again the first priest asks: "What, forsooth, is the sun-like light; what sea is there like unto the ocean; what, verily, is higher than the earth; what is the thing whose measure is not known?" The second priest answers: "Brahma is the sun-like light; heaven is the sea like unto the ocean; the god Indra is higher than the earth; the measure of the cow is unknown." Again the first priest says: "I ask thee for the highest summit of the earth; I ask thee for the navel of the universe; I ask thee for the seed of the lusty steed; I ask thee for the highest heaven of speech." The second priest replies:

"This altar is the highest summit of the earth; this sacrifice is the navel of the universe; this *soma* [i.e. the intoxicating sacrificial drink] is the seed of the lusty steed [i.e. the god Indra]; this Brahman priest is the highest heaven [i.e. the highest exponent] of speech." Such expressions show that the old nature gods were no longer a living reality to the poet. The thinkers knew that there were no deities corresponding to the many names of many gods who had once been adored and believed in. The thinkers were absorbed in searching for the ultimate, invisible reality behind all visible phenomena. In the 164th hymn of the first book of the Rig Veda there are fifty-two lines, all except one of which are riddles, but without any answers. The riddles are about the phenomena of the universe, about heaven and earth, the sun and moon, air, clouds, and rain; about the year, the seasons, months, days, and nights; about the human voice, self-consciousness, life, and death; about the origin of the first creature, and the originator of the universe. The implied suggestion is that above and behind the multitude of gods there is only one.

Though the beginnings of such theosophic speculation started in connection with the sacrifices, yet thought turned more and more to the whence, why, what, and whither of all subjects, especially the mysteries of the universe and human life. While to ask such questions is natural and may be helpful, yet the result shows that such speculation was harmful when not made with a desire and an attempt to fit men to meet the duties of life, but simply to secure metaphysical consistency. The outcome of an immense amount of acute thinking by a large body of quick-witted men ended in a consistent impersonal monism which has not helped men to love God and brother men, but to take a pessimistic view of life and to neglect their duties. The last hymn of the tenth book of the Rig Veda, the 129th, is one of the most remarkable productions of the Indian mind. It expresses the climax of the Vedic pantheism, and well illustrates the religious uselessness of what Indian thinkers had come to consider the height of religious wisdom. It is sometimes called the Creation Hymn, because it expresses the Indian thinker's conclusion about the beginning of all things. A Sanskrit scholar, Dr. John Muir, thus translates it: "There was neither non-entity nor entity, there was no atmosphere, nor sky above. What enveloped (all)? Where, in the receptacle of what (was it contained)? Was it water, the profound abyss? Death was not then, nor immortality; there was no distinction of day or night. That One breathed calmly, self-supported; there was nothing different from or above it. In the beginning darkness existed, enveloped in darkness. All this was undistinguishable water. That One which lay void and wrapped in nothingness was developed by the power of fervour. . . . Who knows, who can declare, whence has sprung, whence this creation? The gods are subsequent to the development of this (universe); who then knows whence it arose? From what this creation arose, and whether any one made it or not—he who in the highest heaven is its ruler, he verily knows, or (even) he does not know." The conclusion of Vedic philosophical speculation is that in the universe there is only one substance which is impersonal and which is rightly termed It or That. This was perhaps the supreme illustration of the sad truth of the apostle's word, "The world by its wisdom knew not God"; "professing themselves to be wise, they became fools." Yet they were seeking God and God was seeking them. This was the first great experience in India of the easy, but awful, fall which comes to the pride of mere intellectualism in religion when divorced from the heart. Yet this metaphysical conclusion of absolute unity in the universe must have given some satisfaction to Indian thinkers; otherwise it could not have remained as it has for over three thousand years the last word of Indian speculation.

But on our assumption that the living God has always been seeking His Indian children, and that they have ever been groping after Him, we may be sure that for the majority of Indians this cold, pantheistic abstraction was not the essence of religious thought and life. It must have been the conclusion of the philosophers alone which they called religion. Even late Vedic literature gives traces of a rising, incipient monotheism. A hymn very near the pantheistic Creation hymn teaches that there is a personal god named Prajāpati, the lord of all creatures. And other late hymns of the Rig Veda show the thinkers' sense of need of a personal interpretation of the universe by likening it to a giant man, called Purusha, and again conceiving of the object of devotion as a personal god called Brihaspati or Brahmanaspati, meaning the lord of prayer or devotion. Also, as in the Greek and Roman religions, so in Hinduism, virtues such as love and wisdom, and abstract conceptions such as time, are semi-personified and then adored. The religious heart of the Indian could not remain satisfied with an impersonal universe. God spoke to the Hindu through the longings of his heart for a personal god to whom he could pray. Though consistent Hindu speculation makes the ultimate Reality of the universe an impersonal monism, doubtless Hindus long ago did what many Hindus now do, viz.: think and speak as if the ultimate It were a person with a loving, gracious heart.

We now pass from the Vedic period to

that of the Upanishads, which are mainly speculations on fundamental questions. They are considered the most important part of the Vedanta, i.e. the close of the Vedas or sacred writings. Yet these Upanishads profess to be the inspired and authoritative interpretations of the four Vedas. In fact the assumptions and conclusions of these philosophical writings differ greatly from those of the books which they profess to interpret. For even where some sacred book is theoretically supposed to be the final authority in religion, as a matter of fact the appeal to life is truly the supreme test. So the facts of life led multitudes of Indians and some of the best thinkers to disregard the teachings of the Vedas and the speculations of the Vedanta school, and to hold to personal and human conclusions in their religious thought and practice.

Death has been a perpetual stimulant to thought and reverence. As Job asked, "If a man die, shall he live again?" so Indians from the earliest times have thought about the mystery of what happens to the one who dies. In many ways these ancient Indians showed their belief in some continuation of the spirit. Weapons and utensils were buried with the corpse. Even when a corpse was burned, for a length of time, at certain dates, offerings are made to the *manes* of the departed. Paradises of various gods were commonly conceived to which souls went in the next world. Retribution and reward were looked for.

But endless retribution and reward for a brief life in this world did not seem just or probable. So speculation turned to one of the most controlling ideas of Hinduism, viz.: re-birth and re-death through many cycles, i.e. to transmigration. That re-birth and re-death are haunting conceptions natural to man is shown by belief in some kind of transmigration in other lands than India. Even among primitive men there has been widely held a belief that not only man, but also animals, plants, and some inanimate objects have souls. That such souls or lives leave the bodies which they have tenanted is apparent. That they re-enter other bodies seems not improbable. In dreams and hallucinations men think that they have knowledge of the departed. Naturally the condition of one's future existence is assumed to depend on one's character in a previous state. Under such natural tendencies, since light and immortality had not then been brought to light through the gospel of Christ, in some inferential way Indians came to believe in transmigration, and in its accompanying doctrine of Karma. The doctrine of Karma is that one's present state of existence is absolutely and exactly the fruit of his actions or character in a previous state of existence, and his state in the next stage will be exactly the fruit of his actions or character in the present stage.

In this conception, with all its error and unsatisfactoriness, we can see both the influence of a righteous God and the dimness of vision of His Indian children. For the Karma doctrine is India's chief response to conscience. In some respects it was an upward movement in religion, because this doctrine recognizes man as having some measure of personality. The Karma-transmigration doctrine also recognizes a moral connection between man's character in one stage of existence and the next. Yet despite this moral value and this assurance of continued existence, the doctrine of transmigration has not been satisfying to the best minds of India. How this is so will be analyzed in the third lecture. The good news of God's gracious help to the weak and erring, which is the chief revelation of the Christ, had not then become known to Hindus. So in the Karma-transmigration doctrine Indian thinkers thought out the most thorough-going and far-reaching doctrine of retribution which any religion has ever taught. But, because it made absolute, unavoidable retribution the only object of this world, and in its consistency left no room for grace, the Indian mind revolted, and one of the two most momentous and sweeping religious changes that have ever occurred took place in India.

In the sixth century B.C., doubtless under the influence of the divine Spirit, there arose in India a new religious leader to protest against the two most unsatisfactory features of the religion then prevalent in India. These evils were, first, an unethical ceremonial and sacrificial system, and second, an unethical and depressing intellectualism. The new religious teacher was Gautama, who was afterwards called the Buddha or enlightened one. After twelve years of dissipation he devoted himself to the study of religion. Finding the teaching of the Brahmans unsatisfactory, he devoted himself to rigorous asceticism. Finding asceticism vain, he resolved by meditation to discover the secret of life and of the universe. After long contemplation he believed that he had discovered the cause of misery and the means of counteracting it. He had come to see that the essence of true religion is not in ceremonials, not in asceticism, not in speculation, but in possessing spiritual characteristics and in living a good life. When he clearly saw this he was termed the enlightened one, the Buddha, and he rightly and immediately sought to do his utmost to let his light shine and to lead others to follow the better way which he called "the middle way," i.e. the mean between mechanical ceremonialism and arid intellectualism. According to the Buddha, on the one hand religion is not, as the priests taught, painful and endless repetitions of ceremonies and sacrifices, nor on the other hand is religion, as the thinkers taught, speculation as to what am I? whence have I come? whither do I go? what is the meaning of the universe? is there or is there not a god? if there is a god, is he personal or impersonal? is he outside or inside the universe, or is he only It?

The Buddha was right in saying that in religion, not ceremonials, nor speculation, but a pure heart and a simple, kindly life are the important things. But when he tried to point out the way by which the pure heart and the simple life are to be secured, he misunderstood the meaning of life. According to the Buddha there are four simple principles for the middle or true way of religion, viz.: first, belief that misery always accompanies existence; second, the cause of misery is desire; third, misery can be escaped only by the cessation of desire; fourth, desire can be escaped by following what is sometimes called the four-fold and sometimes the eight-fold path, the essence of which is a pure heart and a pure life. The teaching of the Buddha was an upward movement for both religious thinking and life.

While the Buddhist reform is one of the greatest illustrations of the might of ideas, perhaps the most impressive lesson of that whole movement is the power of a noble person, who illustrates in his life the purer ideal which he teaches. In the history of the world next to the instance of the Christ, Gautama Buddha is the most impressive example of how a religious leader, with a pure ideal to which he conforms, can change the religion and life of myriads for centuries.

Probably the Buddhist religion is also the most painfully impressive example of how a great movement with a great leader can, from its inspiring beginning, be degraded into mechanical lifelessness, and of how inadequate is any religion which has no adequate conception and living revelation of God. Christians have not always considered the Buddhist revolt against Brahmanism as more or less due to the help of God. But they uniformly consider that a religious reformation in Palestine at almost the same time under the greatest of Hebrew prophets was unquestionably inspired of God. Yet the greater Isaiah was a contemporary of Gautama Buddha. And fundamentally the protests of that Isaiah and of the Buddha were against the same religious evils, viz.: an unethical formalism in religion. Both taught that rites and sacrifices are not true religion, that they are not only of no value in themselves, but on the contrary that, unless springing from a good heart and accompanied by kindness to fellow men, they are evil. Yet one fundamental, far-reaching difference between the teaching of Isaiah and of the Buddha has caused immense difference in the results of the teaching of the two. Isaiah was inspired by the conviction of appointment by a personal God, and he exalted that God. The Buddha had nothing to say about God. Some persons interpret him as denying the existence of God. Others understand that he only disregarded God and sought to make religion merely a morality. That is my opinion. However, the Buddha's teaching, enforced by his own example, that a pure heart and a life of service to fellow men are essentials of true religion, wrought immense good. It greatly lessened the extent and the power of ceremonialism, sacerdotalism, animal sacrifices, the pride of excessive intellectualism and of caste, and promoted simple living and helpfulness to brother men.

But men must pray and must reverence what they deem the divine. So the Buddha had hardly passed away before the arrest and degeneracy of his teachings began. He had distinctly taught that he desired no reverence for himself, but only that all men should attain to truth and to the right goal of their being by following the middle path. However, soon his disciples, and then their followers, and later Buddhists everywhere very considerably misunderstood and misapplied his teachings. Following the easy downward trend of human nature, they began to do the things which he had forbidden, viz.: practically to adore him and to place importance on ceremonies. At first in the worthy effort to serve men and to spread truth, great numbers of Buddhists went far and wide as missionaries. But later, the chief aim of the most devoted Buddhists came to be to abjure the world and to live for themselves. Monks and nuns were deemed to be the most holy men and women. So long as missionary zeal and activity remained in Buddhism, the system retained virility. Like all religions, Buddhism developed differing and somewhat warring sects. An additional fatal defect in Buddhism was holding to the Brahmanical doctrine of Karma and transmigration. In Buddhism the absence of any recognition of God prevents the possibility of worship and true prayer, and the Karma system practically takes motive and inspiration out of life. Those two fatal deficiencies and the downward pull of the flesh brought to Buddhism the usual cycle of arrest, degeneracy, and vain attempts at reform. In a thousand years Buddhism attained practical Nirvana in the land of its birth. There are to-day in India proper more Indian Christians than Buddhists.

At about the same period, probably in the sixth century B.C., there arose, under a leader known as Mahāvira, a religious movement allied to Buddhism, known as Jainism. That two such efforts protesting against Brahmanism developed nearly simultaneously shows the legitimate and widespread dissatisfaction with the excessive ceremonialism of the priests and the excessive intellectualism of the thinkers. At its beginning the appeal and power of Jainism lay in its emphasis on two great truths, the duty of refraining from injuring life in any form, and the rewarding value of a simple life. Non-injury to even humble animal life has always been the prominent doctrine of the Jain religion. Very likely it was the practice of excessive animal sacrifices current when Mahāvira started the Jain movement that made the doctrine of non-injury the principal element in this religion. We believe that it is the influence of God which makes men more considerate to animals to-day than they once were. Why not believe that it was He who helped the founder of the Jain system to his emphasis on kindness to animals? And why was it not from God that the impulse for a simple and kindly life came to Mahāvira? Then why did arrest and degeneracy come to this Jain religion? The same reasons that brought those experiences to other religions. Theologically there are the same two fatal defects in Jainism that there are in Buddhism, viz.: the absence of recognition of, and reverence for a personal God, and the doctrine of metempsychosis. Where there is not a clear adequate conception of a personal, righteous, loving God, the world does not get a right conception of man, and where there is an inadequate conception of man, there is an inadequate conception of God. Where these defects exist arrest, degeneracy, ceremonialism, sacerdotalism must and do come. Thus, while the Jain community in India numbers about a million, that is, about one-third as many as Indian Christians, and while, as a class, they are wealthy, their religion is one of formalism and is unprogressive, with no missionary zeal or effort, and, therefore, it has no appreciable value for India or the world.

From ten to fifteen centuries stretch across the interval from the animism of the aborigines to the ethical revival of religion by the Buddha. Ten centuries cover the period from the rise of Buddhism till its practical disappearance from the land of its birth. How many vicissitudes religion underwent in those millenniums! One's spirit will be hopeful or depressed according to his conception of God. One, like the writer, who has an abiding conviction that God has ever been what the Christ revealed Him to be, the Father of the spirits of all men, will believe that God has always done all that at any time He wisely could for every human child, and has mercifully borne with human limitations, mistakes, and sins. Such a believer will more than ever revere the sublime patience of the all-powerful One to whom a thousand years are as one day, and will feel sure that there is coming a day which will be as a thousand years in its fruition of God's long, paternal search for men, and men's pathetic groping after God. Those who have an exhilarating, grateful experience of what the Christ is doing for their own lives will more earnestly sympathize with their brothers who, without Christ's aid, stretch eager hands to God and who in their search often marvellously sacrifice personal comfort. Such Christians will gladly and eagerly labour to hasten the day of the Lord Jesus Christ, the fulfiller of all partial intimations of God, the author and the finisher of the faith of all men. Indeed not only all Indian Christians, but also not a few broad-minded non-Christians in India are appealing to Christian missionaries to help in sympathetically, and therefore in correctly and hopefully, interpreting the religions of India, and in giving to them and their countrymen the Christian interpretation of life. The most sympathetic interpreters of God's dealings with men have always been, and must always be, the most hopeful of His co-workers.

II

AN INTERPRETIVE OUTLINE OF INDIA'S LATER RELIGIOUS HISTORY

IN the former lecture there was attempted a brief interpretive outline of India's earlier religious history from pre-Aryan times till the rise and decay of the Buddhist and Jain religions. It was claimed that four words epitomized the characteristics of the history of thought and life in India, viz.: progress, arrest, degeneracy, and reform, repeated over and over again. It was assumed that all progress is due to the inspiration of God, because He is the prime agent in all upward movements, and that the repeated arrest and degeneracy in the various religions of India have been due to a struggle of the flesh against the spirit, such as has been carried on in every religion, including the Christian, in which the flesh often gains the victory. I hope that that review of India's earlier religious history justified and illustrated the assumptions underlying this course of lectures. An interpretive outline of India's later religious history, covering about eleven centuries, may be still more satisfying.

In the sixth century B.C. there began two notable protests against the ceremonialism and excessive intellectualism of the priests and against the unbrotherliness of caste, viz.: Buddhism and Jainism. At first both had some enthusiasm for humanity and were missionary organizations and efforts. But both soon suffered arrest and degeneracy. Both largely became ceremonial and formal. Both gave excessive value and prominence to doctrines as the marks of their truth and excellence, while showing less spiritual interest in the betterment of the world. Both became less inspirational for lives of kindly service to fellow men. The Jain religion has continued to the present day, and has about a million adherents. But it is unprogressive and cannot be reckoned an important religious force for India or the world. Buddhism had real value for the world, and therefore spread far through eastern and southern Asia, and still retains influence in some large areas. Yet, though once becoming the paramount religion in India, it suffered steady decline and after continuing about a thousand years, it practically became lifeless, and now for about fifteen hundred years it has been a dead religion in the land of its birth. There are more Indian Christians in India proper than there are followers of the faith of the Buddha. The few Buddhists who remain in India proper are on the northeast borders toward Thibet and Burma. The town of Buddha Gaya, the place where Gautama became Buddha, i.e. the enlightened one, has for centuries been in the possession of haughty Brahmans, who daily teach and practise the opposite of what the enlightened one taught and practiced.

At the time of the Parliament of Religions in Chicago an earnest Buddhist leader from Ceylon came to the United States and from a good many sympathetic people in this country secured considerable funds, with which he made vain legal efforts to wrest from the possession of Brahmans into the hands of Buddhist managers that sacred starting place of the Buddhist faith. There were practically no Buddhists in India who could, or would, take interest in this pecuniary and legal crusade for the birthplace of their religion. So the funds which were uselessly exhausted in the effort had to come mainly from America.

Modern Hinduism may be said to begin in the eighth century of the Christian era. Indian history sheds painfully little light on the thought and life in the seven centuries preceding the eighth, during which period Buddhism had been declining and was finally replaced by modern Hinduism. Yet many of the ideas and practices of Buddhism have been incorporated into Hinduism. Scholars consider that since the eighth century Hinduism has been a mixture of the superstitious rites of the non-Aryan tribes, of the simple religion of Vedic times, of the pantheistic doctrines of the Upanishads, and of the mild doctrines of Buddhism, all directed by the brain-power of the Brahmans in the marvellous social organization of caste.

In the development of this complex system called modern Hinduism the laws of human evolution have ever been at work, and those laws are essentially the two-fold ones of, first, the power of God at work drawing the human spirit toward Himself, and second, the lower tendencies of mankind pulling men's thoughts and lives downward. The lower tendencies of man appear in the superstitious and sensual elements which make up almost the whole of the non-Aryan religions; in the pride of excessive intellectualism, which has made many thinkers lose a sense of reality in life, while straining after metaphysical consistency; in the spirit-killing literalism and pride of ceremonialism in the priests, and in the iron-clad, unprogressive caste system. The uplifting and renewing spirit of God appears in the earnest search for ultimate reality, in the conviction that by loving devotion to a personal God the believer is saved, and in the noble charity which characterized early Buddhism.

Under the Brahmans and some lower-caste leaders, when Hinduism sought to become, and practically did become, a national religion, it had to provide religious ideas and ceremonies for the non-Aryan, as well as the Aryan sections of the people; and there has gradually been a larger and larger mixture of those races. Some ethnologists estimate that now there are not more than five per cent. of pure Aryans in India. Therefore it is not strange that, as in Israel when Solomon and other kings took wives from the non-Jewish peoples, those women brought into the royal court and into the temple the religions of the peoples from whom they had come, so in India, when the races lived side by side and more or less intermingled, their religions also should coalesce. Therefore, as stated in the former lecture, among the sixty millions of people who are pure or nearly pure descendants of the aborigines there still exist many of the ideas and practices of the pre-Aryan religions, and these characteristics have also considerably blended with the beliefs and customs of the masses and even of the intelligent classes. Hence tree worship, and respect for various symbols of creative power, and manifold superstitions and impure practices are common among many of the multitudinous sects of modern Hinduism. The simple religion of Vedic times made its contribution to the Hinduism of the present period by the assumption, generally accepted by most sects, that the Vedas are the final authority in religious matters. The simple masses have been encouraged to continue to ask from many gods the same material blessings which the early Aryans sought. The thinkers of the pantheistic school felt the old necessity of absolute unity in the explanation of the universe, and for themselves, accepted an impersonal monism, while recognizing that the masses must have a personal god to whom they could pray. Under the influence of Buddhism, animal sacrifice greatly lessened, and especially the spiritual equality of all men was recognized and considerably practised. In consequence, for the last twelve hundred years many of the reformers and saints of Hinduism have been men of other than Brahman caste.

In the period now under consideration, namely, from the eighth to the nineteenth century, the first apostle who helped to make modern Hinduism what it is was a Brahman of Central India named Kumārila. The source of his power was an attack on the weakest point of Buddhism. The Buddha never spoke of God. Kumārila placed emphasis on the existence and activity of an all-powerful god as the cause of the existence, continuance, and dissolution of the world. From whom did this reformer get that conviction of a god at work among men, if not from God Himself? Kumārila bequeathed religious leadership to his great disciple S'ankara, who probably lived in the latter part of the eighth century.

Next to the Buddha this S'ankara is the most influential religious teacher who ever lived in India. More than any other man, he is the maker of modern Hinduism. Yet, like our Lord, he died when he was only a little over thirty years of age. His chief intellectual work in Hinduism was the perfecting and popularizing the doctrine of the unity of the divine. Not more insistent or active in preaching the unity of the divine was Mohammed than was S'ankara. On intellectual Hinduism for twelve centuries this man impressed the doctrine of impersonal monism. Yet he also taught the need for men generally of a personal God. Of his influence Sir William Hunter says: "It is scarcely too much to say that since his short life in the eighth or ninth century every new Hindu sect has had to start with a personal god. He addressed himself to the high-caste philosophers on the one hand and to the common multitude on the other. He left behind as the two-fold result of his life's work a compact Brahman sect and a popular religion." For the intelligent Brahman S'ankara taught that there is but one supreme and inscrutable first cause to be worshipped, not by sacrifice, but by meditation. For the common man he allowed the worship of any god, but preferably Shiva, by any rites prescribed by the Vedas or by any later teacher who was deemed orthodox. Especially he developed one of the two popular forms of modern Hinduism, the Shiva cult.

The principle of accommodation carried to excess by S'ankara and by Hindu leaders to this day is one main cause of the power and of the weakness of Hinduism. Probably in no religion in the world is it open to any follower so freely to think as he will, and so freely to worship and live as he will, with one most stringent exception, viz.: he absolutely must not disregard caste regulations. This attempt by an exceptionally acute and forceful man to validate an esoteric religion for thinkers on one principle, and to validate for the masses an exoteric religion inconsistent with the controlling principle of the first system, has never done either class genuine service. It tends to make the thinkers cold-hearted, hypocritical, proud. It prevents the masses from getting from the more gifted class the enlightenment, sympathy, and respect which they need, and tends to push them farther into superstition and formality. This is another illustration of how an upward movement in Hinduism suffered arrest and degeneracy.

S'ankara and his Vedantic school felt the need of unity in an explanation of the universe. They thought that they had found such unity in the Karma transmigration doctrine, by which the past is absolutely controlling for the future, and by which the world is to be deemed unreal. On this assumption, metaphysical consistency led them to accept impersonal monism as the explanation of everything. Yet because man's heart craves, and must have a personal god, these pantheistic thinkers allowed and popularized a personal god. For lack of true belief in a personal god and for lack of a perfect human incarnation of the divine, such as the Lord Jesus Christ is, they were quite content to let the masses believe what they themselves believed to be unreal, and to sink lower and lower into ignorance of truth and into unethical practices. In Buddhism there had been neglect of the soul—the soul of the universe, i.e. God, and neglect of a genuine soul in man because the transmigration idea does not give room for a loving free agent. The Vedantic school went to the opposite extreme and was supremely interested in the metaphysics of the supreme Spirit and its relation to the universe and to human beings. The weakness and nemesis of this system lay in its neglect of the human heart and conscience as the most important factors in religion.

By contrast, the strength of the Hebrew and Christian religions has been their emphasis on a personal, righteous, loving God, who influences the heart and conscience of men to live ethical lives of service. Oh, if the Buddha and if S'ankara had known a personal God, who is the Father of the spirits of all human children, and if, in view of that Father's attitude to His children, those leaders had made loving service of brother men the way of life for all who would be filial to their divine Father, how different would have been the religious history of their country! But the fulness of time for India had not then come.

S'ankara and his followers gave to the masses the Shiva cult, which has since been one of the two chief religions of modern India. In accordance with the principle of excessive accommodation, Shiva was to be to each worshipper that which the worshipper sought. He had a two-fold aspect, one philosophical, in which he is engaged in profound thought, is both the Destroyer and Reproducer of everything, and the emblem of reproduction is his special symbol;

the other aspect is one which makes him and his goddess Kāli, objects of terror, awakening fear in men and stimulating them to efforts for propitiation. Similarly the ritual and worship of Shiva is two-fold. For the higher classes the worship is one of meditation without rites. For the masses, Shiva and Kāli worship is one which requires countless offerings and sacrifices. Later in this lecture I shall describe what till now are the sad features of one large section of the Shivaite religion.

When the Shaiva religion came into the unsatisfactoriness of its two-fold development we might anticipate that, under the influence of God, some protest and reform would be made. These began in the Vishnu cult, which became prominent two or three centuries after S'ankara, i.e. in the eleventh and twelfth centuries A.D. This Vaishnava religion is now one of the two principal religions of India. Life and history are robbed of value by the doctrine of an impersonal monism and its accompanying doctrine of Karma and transmigration. The experience of life discredits such a system. So, as I believe under God's influence, there arose a truer and more helpful form of religion, which is called the way of salvation by loving devotion to a personal god, i.e. the *bhaktimarga.*

While this type of religion was specially popularized and spread from the twelfth century on, its beginnings were long before that time. The most important religious book of India, the Bhagavad Gita, i.e. the Divine Song, inculcates this kind of religion. Scholars believe that this poem, as we have it, has been edited and added to, like other ancient religious books. Its earlier part was composed some centuries before the Christian era. Through additions and modifications it now represents a poem completed some centuries after the Christian era. So it does not contain one consistent teaching. As it stands, it probably shows an attempt to modify a religion of faith in a personal and ethical deity by additions of a pantheistic nature. Its older and most satisfactory teaching is that a personal deity named Krishna, who manifests himself in the form of a human hero, puts forth spiritual teaching, and demands of his disciple the performance of duty, but above all requires faith, love, and resignation toward himself. By a special act of grace, Krishna reveals himself as the divine one, and promises to his faithful disciple after death admission to his presence and fellowship with himself. Disregarding the pantheistic additions to the Bhagavad Gita, the substance of its doctrine of salvation by loving devotion to god is substantially as follows: There is a god who is a conscious, eternal, almighty being. The souls of men are distinct from God and are imperishable. All of God's actions are for the good of the universe. Sin often grows rampant among men. Therefore, whenever justice declines and injustice increases, God assumes new phenomenal forms for the protection of the good and the destruction of the evil, in order to establish the right. The relation of God to the world and men is not, as assumed by the Karma school, solely determined by the law of retribution, but by love to those who know Him and are sincerely devoted to Him. He delivers from sin those who take refuge in

Him. So salvation comes by the grace of God.

The substance of the older part of this poem and its chief religious teachings are unquestionably older than the Christian era and therefore cannot have been borrowed from the New Testament, as some persons have imagined from its similarity to the Christian teaching of salvation by the grace of God's influence on the hearts of those who practice loving devotion to Him. Must we not ascribe this belief and this teaching to the influence of God's Spirit? Is it strange that the Bhagavad Gita is a book much prized and read by modern Hindus? Yet this elevated teaching has been sadly handicapped by the pantheistic additions which confuse its teaching and which hinder Hindus from understanding and accepting its best spiritual elements.

The poem is further weakened by a defect in its practical teaching. In it two ways of salvation are given and contrasted. One way, like that of pantheistic Hinduism, consists in withdrawal from the world and search for knowledge by meditation. The other way consists in actions conformable to duty, but free from desire. The poem plainly teaches that the old Hindu idea is correct, which teaches that a true salvation is deliverance from the cycle of existence, to be secured by meditation in isolation from the world; yet that there is also a second way of salvation, viz.: by right actions performed without a desire for reward. This confusing two-fold doctrine and the philosophical cast of the poem prevent it from being like the Bible, a plain, understandable book both for the uneducated and the educated.

So, while the doctrine of salvation by loving devotion began some centuries before Christ and received formal exposition in a remarkable poem, yet the widespread acceptance of the doctrine began in the twelfth century A.D. through the influence of a Brahman reformer in Southern India, named Rāmānuja. He revolted from the thoroughgoing impersonal monism of S'ankara, and introduced a more human type of religion. The philosophy of Rāmānuja was a modified monism or a qualified idealism. He taught that God, whom he usually spoke of and worshipped as Vishnu, is a personal being, and that the human soul has real and distinct entity, though after death its goal is absorption into Vishnu, while the way of salvation is by loving devotion to God, i.e. *bhakti*. Since the somewhat allied Christian doctrine of salvation by faith was unquestionably developed in Europe under the influence of God's Spirit, why is it not right to assume that this protestant reform in the Hindu religion was also prompted by God? While this according of some measure of personality to deity and of some real existence to the human soul was an upward move, of still greater value was the doctrine of Vaishnavism that the soul is not only personal, but moral, that it is not only ignorant, but sinful, and that its salvation is to be obtained not by merit, but by the grace of God through loving devotion to Him.

The influence of Rāmānuja, the first leader of Vaishnavism, was among the upper classes, of which he, as a Brahman, was a member. About two hundred years later, in the fourteenth century, there lived another reformer named Rāmānanda who carried throughout a large part of India this doctrine of salvation through loving devotion to a personal God. He is considered the fifth great Vaishnava leader in succession to Rāmānuja. Besides preaching the doctrine and power of *bhakti,* Rāmānanda went beyond previous leaders in making this faith familiar with the masses, and he chose his twelve disciples, not from priests or nobles, but from the common people and even from the despised classes. One of these disciples was a leather-worker, another a barber, and the most distinguished was the son of a weaver. In India Rāmānanda was a contemporary of Wyckliffe in Britain. Both the British Christian reformer and the Indian Hindu reformer sought to purify religion by making it a personal experience dependent on right relation to God, and not on a hierarchy. Why should not the one, as well as the other reformer, be gratefully counted as taught and strengthened by God?

The religion in which *bhakti* was the chief element is known, not only as Vaishnavism, but also as the Bhāgavata religion, the beginnings of which may be traced to Vedic times. There was a Vedic deity named Bhaga, who was considered the bestower of blessings. Gradually the word *bhaga* came to be the word for goodness and not the name of a god. Then, according to the laws of the Sanskrit language, the name of a god of goodness came to be Bhagavat, i.e. the divine possessor of goodness. Then, by another linguistic derivation, the worship of the god Bhagavat was termed the Bhāgavata religion. In the epic poem the Mahābhārata, this Bhāgavata religion is named, and since that poem in its present form was known at least as early as four centuries before Christ, this Bhāgavata religion is older than the Christian religion. Yet because the chief doctrine of this religion, viz.: salvation by the grace of God received by any one who exercises faith or loving devotion to Him, is an approximation to the Christian doctrine of salvation by faith, some Christians have inferred that this system must somehow have been borrowed from the Christian religion. For two reasons this inference is unwarranted. The first reason is conclusive:

The beginnings of the *bhakti* doctrine unquestionably can be found in India some centuries before the Christian era in the Bhagavad Gita. The second reason is a probable one, namely, almost all the doctrines of the Christian religion have their counterparts in some phases of Hinduism, and this is not strange, but natural, because the divine Spirit who taught these truths to Christians was never inactive toward non-Christians. Moreover, the Christ distinctly said that He came to fulfil the earlier teachings of God, and He did not come to teach new doctrines, so much as to give a dynamic for true living. Yet it is a historical fact that the first wide prevalence of this Bhāgavata religion, of which the doctrine of salvation by grace to whoever exercises loving devotion to any god, is the main doctrine, became widespread in India from the fourteenth century of the Christian era. And when this religious system became prevalent it was mainly through preachers and saints of the humbler classes, even through some eminent and saintly women.

In this connection it is illuminating and

instructive to note that on the doctrine of divine grace modern Bhāgavatas are divided into two schools of thought which are respectively influential in the north and in the south of India. The North school teaches that God's gracc is co-operative, i.e. that school advocates the necessity of human freedom and co-operation in the appropriation of salvation. The South school teaches that God's grace is irresistible. The names given to the two schools from their peculiar doctrines about the manner in which grace is secured by the believer well illustrate the Indian way of thinking. The North school's doctrine that the grace of God is obtained only when the believer co-operates with God in the appropriation of His grace is called "The monkey way," because, as the infant monkey itself clings to its mother and co-operates with its parent in receiving her help, so the worshipper must actively co-operate with the deity when receiving from Him the grace which comes from loving devotion. The doctrine of the South school of Bhāgavatas is called "The cat way," because, as the kitten wholly surrenders itself to be carried by its mother, so the worshipper in exercising *bhakti* is wholly passive to the grace of God. According to this southern school the result of loving devotion of the worshipper is the irresistible grace of God toward that devotee. It is an interesting coincidence that, as in Europe the Northern Christians were advocates of human freedom and responsibility, so in Northern India pious Hindus taught co-operative grace on the part of the believer when exercising faith, while both in Southern Europe and Southern India the advocates of salvation by faith held the doctrine of irresistible grace.

Another good element in this Bhāgavata religion was a doctrine which practically taught the separate immortality of the soul, something quite different from the absorption of the spirit into the infinite It. It was taught that when the Infinite put forth the individual soul as a separate existence it is to remain forever as a conscious separate being. However, the Bhāgavata religion had a limited acceptance of the Hindu idea of transmigration, so far that the soul has its round of deaths and re-births until saved by *bhakti*. Yet when the soul develops *bhakti* it is released from re-births and enjoys a perpetual conscious, independent existence at the feet of God. There its blessing is serving and waiting on Him. The soul does not become Him, but becomes like Him, and so remains in everlasting conscious bliss. The doctrine of sin in this Bhāgavata religion is also an improvement over the doctrine of sin in ordinary Hinduism. According to this school, sin is any act at variance with loving devotion to God. Every such sin deserves and should receive the legitimate punishment of its natural fruits. Yet the adorable one graciously forgives his loving disciple.

Another influential element of the Bhāgavata religion was the doctrine of incarnations. The idea of a god becoming incarnate is a very old one in India. In old Vedic literature there are stories that now one god and now another became incarnate to save the gods or to conquer the world. But finally this incarnation idea was detached from other gods and became specially connected with stories of the alleged incarnation of Vishnu in connection with the Bhāgavata religion. It was natural. Vishnu was a personal god with many human characteristics, ready to show grace to men in trouble. The heart longed for a concrete object to which to turn in loving devotion. The heart believes that a great God will be ready to lay aside privilege in order to help needy worshippers. Christians believe that in the Lord Jesus Christ there was a perfect incarnation of the divine in a human form. Why may not God have led the pious Hindu also to believe in God's readiness to empty Himself and take a lowly form in order to help His needy children, even though the alleged incarnations of Vishnu are inadequate and even grotesque specimens of what would seem worthy incarnations of the divine? At any rate the doctrine of incarnation developed in the Bhāgavata religion more than elsewhere in Hinduism, and the most popular of the nine past incarnations of Vishnu are the two in which he is said to have assumed real human forms, viz.: Rāma and Krishna.

The stories of Rāma rarely imply unworthy characteristics. At the beginning the beliefs in Krishna's incarnation were lofty, as is seen from the character which he bears in the Bhagavad Gita. But the tendency of the human mind to take a downward path is perhaps most sadly illustrated in the degeneracy of the Krishna mythology. Apart from the historical fact that the oldest story about Krishna reaches a high ethical plane, there is the certainty that the reverence of men nowhere can be secured at first for an unworthy character. Our Lord's teaching that the upward way is difficult, while the downward road is easy, simply expresses the principle of which the history of Hinduism is one of the clearest and most impressive illustrations that degeneracy in religion is easy and common. A powerful and luxuriant imagination is the most prominent mental power of the Hindu. From early times till to-day the Hindu uses language which seems to the occidental extravagant and sensuous. Erotic language does not necessarily imply impure thoughts in Hindu literature more than in the Song of Solomon. So the highly sensuous and erotic language applied to

Krishna in the later Puranic literature does not at the *beginning* seem to have implied immorality on Krishna's part. But ere long the flesh pulled down the spirit, and sooner or later the masses took these stories of the Krishna incarnation as indicating that he was a licentious and immoral character. How God must have mourned over these numerous and sad aberrations and degeneracies of religion!

Almost certainly the incarnation doctrine of the Bhāgavata religion did not tend to destroy polytheism. It may have strengthened that tendency. At any rate polytheism has always been associated with the Bhāgavata system, as in all other Hindu systems. This may have been one fruit of the principle of excessive accommodation. Polytheism in India is certainly one result of pantheism. If everything is divine and the divine is everything, all distinctions are unreal. Then why should not men regard some places and powers which attract special attention as certainly divine and worship them!

One of the next developments of the Bhāgavata religion was the importance given to the religious teacher or guru. Even in the Christian religion and certainly in every other religion the ordinary man feels the need of a guide in spiritual things, as well as in medicine, and travel, and all relations of life. But probably no religion emphasizes the need of a spiritual guide so much as Hinduism. Also one of the finest characteristics of Hindus is what has been called their genius for recognizing and following a helpful religious leader. However, as in other respects, so in the Hindu's excessive regard for his guru the lack of proportion is a fatal defect. Extravagant claims for such leaders were soon made, and generally admitted. One of the principal books of the Bhāgavata religion, the *Bhaktamāla,* or String of Saints, in its very first line gives as the essentials of true religion the following four: Faith, the believer, the divine one to be believed in, and the guru. The order of these four essentials makes not God, nor loving devotion to Him, but the religious leader and devotion to him, the most important thing in religion.

In the coming of Islam into contact with

Hinduism the devout man should see the guiding hand of God. Indian pantheism had metaphysically prepared the way for the monotheism of the Mohammedans. But that pantheism had also been a real cause of the unhealthy growth of polytheism, idolatry, and superstition which always develop in the masses when the thinkers pursue pantheism. There must have been need of a stern, iconoclastic religion like Islam which flamed with indignation against these abuses which outwardly appeared to be the whole of Hinduism. The Indian people were far too numerous for these Mohammedan conquerors to offer them *en masse* a choice between the sword or submission to the prophet of Mecca. Yet with a rough hand they often broke down or mutilated temples and smashed idols, and supposed that thereby they were casting out superstition and cleansing religion. The fundamental spiritual inadequacy and defect of Islam is that it has not the controlling, constructive purpose of the Christ. Mohammed's controlling idea was not to fulfil, but to destroy. The Mohammedans did great service for India, but their greatest service was other than that which they intended or understood. Few lessons are fitted to be so suggestive to those who would Christianize India as understanding how Islam most helped India to purify its religion. The religious history of India shows that though considerable numbers of Hindus from the uneducated and lower classes became Mohammedans, the greatest service of Islam was not to make converts, but, without intention, to inspire some devout and thoughtful Hindus to see the fundamental truths of monotheism and to initiate new reforming movements. Because the Mohammedan sway was principally in North India these reforming efforts were mainly made in that part of the country.

Chronologically, several of these important reforms took place in India at the same time that Luther was leading the Protestant Christian Reformation movement in Europe. In general, the cause and the main characteristic of both Christian and Indian reforms was a revolt from the ceremonialism and sacerdotalism, which were becoming burdensome to true religion in both Europe and Asia. The earliest of these reformers who came under the monotheistic influence of Islam was Kabir, who lived and taught near Benares in the early part of the sixteenth century A.D. By birth, Kabir may have been a Mohammedan, but eventually he became a disciple of the Rāmānanda school of the Bhāgavata religion and so is considered a Hindu reformer. He taught that there is, and can be, only one God, that idolatry is folly and sin, that religion is devotion to one god, who he himself worshipped as Vishnu, Rāma, or Hari, or even by the names of god which were current among Mohammedans. His teachings were an attempt to compromise between Hinduism and Islam, and were largely tinged with the basal Hindu pantheistic belief. Kabir made many disciples, who are called Kabirpanthis, not a few of whom are found to-day. The keynote of Kabir's teachings was the duty of every man to search for, and find, and then to obey a spiritual teacher.

But the most influential reforming movement began in the Northwest under Nānak, the first great guru of the Sikhs. Translated into English the word Sikhs means Disciples. Nānak was a contemporary of Luther, and in some respects was like that great German Christian reformer. If we rightly ascribe Luther's movement to inspiration from God, we ought also to do the same for Nānak's. The founder of the Sikh religion wrote a book called the Granth, i.e. *the* book, which contains the principles of his faith, viz.: some measure of the unity and personality of God, the distinctness and responsibility of man, and therefore some degree of real sin. He was almost as severe against polytheism and idolatry as the Mohammedans.

But like all previous reforming movements in India, this Sikh religion suffered arrest and soon suffered degeneracy. The first cause of its arrest was the subtle influence of Hindu pantheism from which Nānak could not free himself. To the Christian worker, perhaps the most impressive lesson from Sikhism is the danger and ineffectiveness of compromise in religion. Truth has many phases and applications. But truth is not something to be compromised. Nānak taught the deceptive principle, which has always been, and still is, most attractive to the Hindu mind, that truth is not absolute, but only what seems to be truth to any one. He tried to combine belief in one personal god with belief in the impersonal It of pantheism; of belief in some personality in man with belief that he is an unreal emanation from the Infinite whose end it is to be reabsorbed into It; of belief that man is a real and responsible sinner with belief that the universe is an illusion ruled by *māyā*. This led to practical denial of free will, and to belief in fate. Thus Nānak said:

> "The power of this one is not in this one's hand.
> The cause of causes is the Lord of all.
> The creature is helpless and must obey.
> What pleases That one, that will be."

According to Sikhism the principal means of attaining salvation are reverence for religious teachers, abundant repetition of the names of deity, and charity to men and animals.

One point in which Sikhism is saner and

more helpful in teaching and influence than ordinary Hinduism, is that it teaches the disciples to stay in the world to help it, instead of fleeing from it. Also Nānak did not teach nor believe in the Hindu caste system. He said: "Thou (O, God), acknowledgest the light (that is in him) and does not ask after his caste." And the tenth and last guru, Guru Govind Singh, commanded that caste should not be recognized in the Sikh community. However, this command has never been fully carried out. Degeneracy began by the practical deification of the guru, by excessive reverence for the sacred book, which is practically worshipped, though the book itself is severe on idolatry, and by formalism, which makes the repetition of divine names a means of spiritual renewal. More and more the Sikh religion has tended to become a sect of Hinduism, and even to-day that tendency is strikingly marked.

Others beside Nānak were influenced by Mohammedanism. Prominent among these were Tulsidās, Chaitanya, and Tukārām, all of whom are classified as Sādhus or saints.

These spiritual-minded men lived in the fifteenth and sixteenth centuries, and to my mind reached the highest development of a pure religion up to their times. Before, and in their times, Hinduism had again become largely one of polytheism, unmeaning ceremonies, fasts, and vows, of a degrading type of sacred books called Purānas, and a mechanical religion. These Sādhus, unquestionably under the influence of God's Spirit, made religion consist of faith in a personal god or gods, in purity of heart awakened by loving devotion, and in simplicity and kindliness of life. Here is one short characteristic poem of Tukārām, the most noted Sādhu of Western India:

"I am a denizen of Vaikuntha, and have come
To bring into practice that which was taught by the Rishis:
We will sweep clean the ways of the sages; the world
Is overgrown with weeds.
We will accept the portion that has remained.

Truth has disappeared in consequence of
the Purānas; ruin
Has been effected by pedantry.
The heart is addicted to pleasures, and
the Way is destroyed.
We will beat the drum of *bhakti,* the terror
of the Kali age.
Says Tukā, raise shouts of victory through
joy."

It is my impression that, while the religious influence of the pious Sādhus was very great, and while it has never lost vitality, yet Hinduism as a whole was only moderately modified by these healthy movements. Superstition, polytheism, idolatry, formalism, unmeaning ceremonies, immorality, characterized a large part of Hinduism. The worship of force, or Shakti, personified as a goddess, and subordinately in all women, became common. In the latest sacred writings called Tantras, Force, personified as a goddess, receives excessive veneration, and this popular Hinduism became a most corrupt and demoralizing form of religion. This personified goddess of Force is usually considered the wife of Shiva, and like him, is the divinity who is the object of superstitious fear. According to Monier Williams, "her many personifications are female fiends or ogresses of repulsive habits." Not long ago the Hon. Gopal Hari Deshmukh, a scholarly Hindu gentleman of Western India, published a book called the Agama-prakāsha, in which he gives extracts from the sacred writings called Tantras, in one of which is the following description of the goddess Kāli, the chief personification of female energy, from whose sacred place on the river Hugli, Kālighata, the city of Calcutta received its name. The Tantra book says: "One should adore with liquors and oblations that Kāli who has a terrible gaping mouth and uncombed hair; who has four hands and a garland formed of the heads of the demons whom she has slain and whose blood she has drunk; who holds a sword in her lotus-like hand; who is fearless and awards blessings; who is as black as the large clouds and has the whole sky for her clothes; who has a string of skulls around her neck, and a throat besmeared with blood;

who wears ear-rings (consisting of two dead bodies); who carries two dead bodies in her hands; who has terrible teeth and a smiling face; whose form is awful and who dwells in burning grounds (for consuming corpses); who stands on the breast of her husband, Mahādeva." Of this Shakti worship of female energy, Monier Williams says: "It might have been expected that a creed which admits of an infinite multiplication of female deities and makes every woman an object of worship would be likely to degenerate into various forms of licentiousness on the one hand, and of witchcraft on the other. But, if such consequences might have been anticipated, the actual fact has been worse than the most gloomy pessimist could possibly have foretold."

Another degrading form of modern Shākta Hinduism is a reproduction of the old and superstitious belief that the mere repetition of sacred texts or mantras has magical power to cause every conceivable good to one's self and evil to one's enemies. Such, and even worse features of popular Hinduism which one cannot well quote, are down to the present day illustrations of the awful depths to which that system had fallen. Caste was iron-clad and repressive. The flesh continued to triumph over the spirit.

But it is darkest shortly before dawn. At such a juncture Christian influences on a considerable scale were brought by God into contact with Hinduism. I now outline some of the results of this contact. The result was the beginning of a new victory of the spirit over the flesh. Its most marked movement was in Calcutta. An intelligent Brahman of noble family, Rājāh Rāmmohan Roy, as a lad had many a discussion with his father on the subject of idolatry. This so disturbed his relations with his parent that he was sent away from home. In pursuit of religious truth he studied Persian and Arabic that he might get first-hand knowledge of religious books in those languages. As a young man he made a perilous journey across the Himalayas to Thibet to study Buddhism at one of its most sacred fountains. Disappointed by the search, he went to Benares to study Sanskrit and Hinduism at its most sacred spot. Becoming reconciled to his father and engaging in business, he studied English and Arabic. In Arabic he carefully studied the Kurān and patiently studied the Bible in English, Hebrew, and Greek. As a result of study, thought, and conferences with thoughtful friends, he taught that there is only one God, who is the father of the spirits of all men; that in all religious movements men were blindly seeking after that God, and therefore that the goal in religion is for all men to agree in the spiritual worship of the one God whom all seek and vaguely acknowledge, accompanied by service to fellow men. He early published a tract entitled "The Precepts of Jesus; Guide to Peace and Happiness." In the preface to that tract he wrote: "This simple code of religion and morality is so admirably calculated to elevate men's ideas to high and liberal notions of One God, who has equally subjected all living creatures, without distinction of caste, rank, or wealth, to change, disappointment, pain, and death, and has equally admitted all to be partakers of the bountiful mercies which He has lavished over nature; and is also so well fitted to regulate the conduct of the human race in the discharge of their various duties to God, to themselves, and society, that I cannot but hope the best effects from its promulgation in the present form." He drew to himself a number of disciples and organized a theistic church called the Brahma Samāj, meaning "the God church or community."

After opposition and persecution, this movement was strengthened by the accession of a second great leader, named Babu Debendranāth Sen, connected with a very wealthy family. After a youth of triviality, Debendranāth became impressed with the vanity of worldly pleasure. Then, in the yearning after a higher life, he joined the Brahma Samāj. But he was disillusioned at finding that, while most of its members were intellectually theists, yet they were not loyal to their conviction in home and public life. So he started a Truth-seeking Society, the members of which bound themselves by a solemn covenant to give up idolatry, and to cultivate a life of prayer and simple service. Then the troublesome question arose as to the basis of authority in religion. As a result of study and discussion the Brahma Samāj adopted a statement embodying the fourteen fundamental beliefs of the movement, of which the first two are as follows:

"I. The book of nature and intuition form the basis of the Brahmic faith. II. Although the Brahmos do not consider any book written by man the basis of their religion, yet they do accept with respect and pleasure any truth contained in any book."

Meanwhile, a third development occurred in the Samāj. A young man of marked ability and spirituality, Keshab Chandar Sen, became a leader in the movement. Then gradually there occurred in the Samāj that which occurs in every living organism, a struggle between the conservative and progressive elements. Keshab pushed for the elimination of caste and unspiritual Hindu elements. But, because the executive was conservative, in 1866 the young minister and the liberal members left the mother church to form a new Samāj with far-reaching, advanced principles. The new movement called itself, "The New Dispensation," the creed of which is short and simple:

"(1) One God, one Scripture, one Church.
(2) Eternal progress of the soul.
(3) Communion of prophets and saints.
(4) Fatherhood and Motherhood of God; brotherhood of man and sisterhood of woman.
(5) Harmony of knowledge and holiness, love and work, Yoga and Asceticism in their highest development.
(6) Loyalty to sovereign."

While this movement was developing in Northeast India, a very similar movement in Western India was organized as the Prārthanā Samāj, or Prayer Church. The principles of this theistic church of Western India are not very unlike the principles of the Christian Church, but with less prominence to the Lord Jesus Christ. It claims that the best thought of Aryan, Semite, and Christian alike has been directed to the evolution of the spiritual aspirations of man; that the duty of every spiritual movement is not to destroy, but to fulfil the highest teaching of preceding teachers; that India is above all countries fitted to be the sphere for a new and finest spiritual religion, because it is her genius to absorb the best from all influences which come to her; that in India the belief that a man must be born again has never been extinguished; that the nature of the new religion, which is to be established, and which has begun in India, will be liberation from a formulated law and acceptance of faith or loving devotion to God as a higher law, by which the carnal in men will be in subjection to the spiritual; that the door to this spiritual kingdom will be repentance; and that mercy and service to men, not ceremonies or sacrifices, will be the fruits of the religion.

Of course such a lofty and simple programme of the theistic churches of India is the fruit of the divine Spirit taking the teachings and example of the Lord Jesus Christ and impressing them upon the best men of that country. The main question is whether, apart from the supremacy which the Christian Church assigns to the Christ, these theistic churches can have the dynamic which history and personal experience show to be unattained without recognizing the Christ as the supreme power of God unto salvation. It would be legitimate to speak of other movements in Hinduism, such as the Arya Samāj and the Theosophical Society, which are less influenced by contact with Christian thought and Western influences. But time does not permit such references.

What does this general review of India's religious history suggest to a Christian lover of India? Does it not justify the forecast that India's history epitomizes the four words: progress, arrest, degeneracy, and reform, repeated over and over again? Does it not indicate the working of God's Spirit in seeking the Indian, and that He has never left Himself without witness? Does it not show a marvellous, patient, continuous groping of the Indian after God, which deserves and should receive more light from God, who is the rewarder of them that diligently seek Him? Especially when we see the wonderful and encouraging change and power that come to spiritual-minded Indians when they come into contact with the Christ, is not the leading impression that India needs the Christ, that she has long been preparing for Him, that she is being greatly drawn to Him, that she is likely more and more to follow, worship, and serve Him, and that when India's best sons accept His loving power, they will prove marvellous interpreters of His character and influence? This will be the subject of the fifth lecture.

III

AN ANALYSIS OF SOME FUNDAMENTALS OF HINDUISM

IN two former lectures there was given a general interpretive outline of the development of India's religious history till the present time. It was assumed that such an outline would show that, as in other lands in connection with other religions, so in India the history of its religious thought and life would be characterized by four terms: progress, arrest, degeneracy, and reform, repeated over and over again; i.e. it would be a striking, epitomized story in a wonderful country of the struggle of the Spirit against the flesh and of the flesh against the Spirit, because God has ever been seeking His Indian children while they have been dimly, and often wrongly, groping after Him; but that the best in religious thought and life has not been realized in

India because her fulness of time to know the supreme revelation of God in His Son, the Lord Jesus Christ, had not come.

In addition to such an outline, a more detailed and close analysis of some fundamental phases of India's religious beliefs and practices is needed to emphasize the position taken, and to prepare the way for the final lecture on India's Preparation for the Christ and Christ's Power to meet that Preparation. It is not necessary to attempt any analysis of lower or popular Hinduism, for, though there is much of the lower Hinduism still in the land, and though for practical purposes Christian missionaries will long have much to do to replace such unsatisfactory religion with Christian doctrine and life, yet confessedly this lower Hinduism is doomed and is passing away.

For centuries not a few representatives of the purer phases of India's thought and life have relentlessly criticised such unsatisfactory religion, and have made efforts to supplant it by better conceptions and better living, and to-day many earnest non-Christian Indians are engaged in the same worthy effort. While the best religious thought and effort of intelligent and earnest non-Christian Indians appreciate the work which Christian missionaries have done in exposing the imperfections and wrongs of popular Hinduism and in working for their removal, yet those non-Christian reformers are naturally undertaking for their ancestral faiths a task similar to that attempted by the Neo-Platonists in the second and third centuries of the Christian era, when the popular religions of Europe, Western Asia, and Northern Africa were passing away, and the more philosophical and ethical followers of the old religions sought to arrest the progress of Christianity by purifying and reinvigorating the older faiths. As in the West the most thoughtful Christians are studying the origins of their own religion, partly to see what unsatisfactory elements have entered into it, and partly to make clearer what are the essentials of the Christian faith, so naturally intelligent Hindus are doing the same for their religion and are seeking to show that the higher Hinduism is a satisfactory religion at least for Indians. Therefore, it is both fitting and necessary that Christian leaders also should seek to study the bases of the higher Hinduism and to interpret their significance.

While Hinduism, unquestionably, is a mixture of many and divergent doctrines and practices, yet undoubtedly there are also a few elements which are characteristic of what may be called entire Hinduism. This lecture is an attempt to interpret two such fundamentals, viz.: first, the belief in Karma and transmigration and release therefrom; and, secondly, caste. Bloomfield expresses the view of all scholars when he says: "A pessimistic view of transmigration and release from transmigration are the true signs of Hinduism in the broadest sense of that word." The idea of transmigration has appeared in many parts of the world. It is uncertain when belief in it began in India. Its earliest source may have been the totemistic belief that when a spirit leaves its body, it joins its totem in another sphere. Scholars say that the earlier forms of Indian monotheistic and monistic speculation show no sign of a belief in transmigration. So, while its beginning may have been in folk-lore, partly or mainly taken from the beliefs of aboriginal races, in its developed form belief in transmigration probably began toward the latter part of the Vedic period, and it is unmistakable in the Upanishad period. In this period it is always connected with the doctrine of Karma. There is some difference of opinion as to whether the Karmic idea strengthened the hold of the earlier transmigration idea, or whether belief in transmigration led to the Karma doctrine.

The doctrine of transmigration * is this: Every living creature is born and re-born in some organic shape; every living creature passes from one to another in a countless series of existences until in some form of existence all desire and all activity as the result of desire have passed. The reason why the soul must thus wander from life to life is, first, that, so long as the soul has any desire, that desire must result in a deed, and

* In this section of this lecture great obligation is acknowledged to "Karma and Redemption" by A. G. Hogg, M. A., of the Madras Christian College.

that deed must have its recompense in some future state of existence; and, secondly, the soul changes its habitation according to the quality of its deeds in the previous state of existence.

The allied doctrine of Karma is defined by Deussen, one of the greatest authorities, as follows: "The idea of Karma is that life, in quality as well as quantity, is the accurately meted and altogether fitting expiation of the deeds of previous existence. This expiation takes place through (*bhoktritvam* and *kartritvam*) enjoying and acting, where the latter is again inevitably converted into deeds which must be expiated anew in a subsequent existence, so that the clockwork of requital in running down winds itself up again; and so on in perpetuity—unless there comes upon the scene the universal knowledge which, as will be seen, does not rest upon merit, but breaks its way into existence without connection therewith, to dissolve utterly, to burn up the seed of deeds and thus to render a continuance of the transmigration impossible forever after. However, knowledge cannot arrest the *present* existence, because the latter is conditioned by the deeds in an earlier birth. Their seed, having already sprung up, has escaped the general destruction, and demands to be completely requited. Death cannot supervene so long as a remnant of deeds from previous existence is left, but whenever this is exhausted, life must go out like a lamp when the oil has been consumed. Upon death those who have not attained knowledge are conducted by fantastic ways to requital in realms beyond and are then brought back into new forms of existence. Those who have attained knowledge are merged in identity with Brahman forthwith, if it be the higher knowledge or, if it be the lower, by the roundabout road of the Devayana, or way of the gods."

The subject of present examination is the idea of Karma and the way of release therefrom. Whether some doctrine of transmigration preceded the distinct articulation of the Karma doctrine or not, it seems probably that the Karma doctrine had more influence in determining the transmigration doctrine than the reverse. The doctrine of

Karma appears to be the plainest doctrine in Hinduism, expressing the response of the Hindu conscience to the voice of God, because the Karmic doctrine is the clearest and most forceful Hindu recognition of the moral order of the universe. However, as we shall soon see, it was such recognition accompanied by serious defects. So, while it was at first a progress upward, it also suffered the arrest of development and then degeneracy, which have so regularly and pathetically characterized Hinduism. Yet the doctrine of the way of release from Karma, which is characteristic of the higher Hinduism, is an effort to limit the error of the Karma doctrine, and is another call of the Hindu heart in darkness for help from the Father of spirits, the satisfying answer to which appeal is, I believe, to come from His Son, the Lord Jesus Christ.

The doctrine of Karma is the answer of the Hindu's intellect and conscience to the age-long, universal problem which seeks an explanation of the mystery of apparently unmerited suffering. Our Lord's disciples propounded that problem to Him when they asked: "Rabbi, who did sin, this man, or his parents, that he should be born blind?" They assumed, as most men in most lands without the Christian solution have assumed, that undeserved suffering must have been caused by some one's sin. Later I shall enlarge on the Christian doctrine that the undeserved sufferings of the Christ are a revelation of the divine heart, showing that unmerited suffering is necessarily bound up with the character of a loving God. He *must* suffer in order to save His children from their sins. Later elucidation will show this to have been the meaning of Christ's answer to the question about the reason of the man's being born blind: "Neither did this man sin, nor his parents, but that the works of God should be manifest in Him." Yet, till the suffering Christ gave the Christian solution to the problem which has always haunted thinkers, even the Old Testament could not give the only measurably satisfying solution to the problem of suffering which the Christ gives.

In the drama of Job the mystery was clearly stated, but not consistently answered to the mental satisfaction of Job or his comforters, or to present-day readers. Like the disciples who assumed that the ultimate cause of the blind man's having been born blind must have been some one's wrong-doing, Job's comforters assumed that, though Job *appeared* to have been a good man, he must have sinned; otherwise God, who must be good, would have been unjust in allowing Job to suffer. Job denied having done any wrong which could deserve such suffering, and was naturally tempted to infer that God had been unjust to him. Without denying the assumptions of both Job and his friends that according to a moral order a man would not be allowed to suffer thus except for sin, the writer of the drama gets out of the difficulty by assuming that suffering is only a mystery, and that Job's experience was exceptional. In the law of Karma, the Hindu thinkers give a theoretically more consistent explanation than the writer of the drama of Job. Their answer to the problem of Job would have been this: both Job and his friends are right in assuming that good conduct must be rewarded by prosperity, and that misfortune implies guilt. Job is right in affirming that he is upright, that is, he has been upright in his present life. His friends are right in assuming that Job's sufferings are due to his having sinned, and though he did not sin in this life, his sufferings must be the result of sins in a former state of existence.

While such a solution by the Hindu thinker would be logically a more consistent answer to the problem of Job than the Old Testament solution, the latter would practically be more helpful. I believe that the reason for the differing solutions is that the Hindu had not a controlling belief in a personal god of moral character. The Old Testament writer had such a god. The Hindu was intellectually more acute and logical, but by his wisdom he knew not God, though that God was impressing his mind with the assurance of a mysterious moral order, which requires that sin and righteousness must be adequately dealt with. The Hebrew knew God, though his logic limped. This was the reason why the Hindu thinker, with much of reason and not a little of morals on his side, has from the first swung more and more away from the highest explanation of the problem of apparently undeserved suffering. Nor will he find it till he accepts the solution which the suffering Christ gives.

However, the Hindu doctrine of Karma, being a reply of both conscience and intellect to the problem which has perplexed all thinking men, has some real moral value. Christians should intelligently and fairly recognize the excellences, as well as the defects of the doctrine, because when the excellence, as well as the defect, is not seen and acknowledged, the former seems, even to some men in the West, a plausible reconciliation of the facts of life with the claims of abstract justice. But when both its excellences and defects are seen, it should appear a preparation for the Christ.

The merits of the doctrine of Karma are as follows: First, it recognizes that a man's lot in this life is not proportioned to his character, and therefore, that there must be somewhere an explanation and righting of this apparent injustice. Secondly, it emphasizes the connection of cause and effect in morals as in the other affairs of the universe. While it will later be shown that the theory overlooks the undeniable fact that the fruit of a man's sins are not, and cannot be, borne *only* by himself, yet it does rightly teach that even a single sin of any man has momentous importance and that every sin of every man must somehow be expiated; also that the consequence of an act is really not a separate thing, but is a part of the act itself. Also, while another weakness in the theory will be pointed out later, that it overlooks the most solemn result of sin, viz.: that the greatest injury of sin is not that it *brings* a resultant curse, but *is,* in itself, the worst curse, yet it is important to remember that the universal tendency of sin is to bring a curse. Thirdly, it is an excellence in the Karmic doctrine that by teaching that the wrongdoer must himself unavoidably eat the fruit of every single evil deed, it emphasizes the inference that he cannot expiate his demerit by any amount of meritorious deeds. The Christian who believes in salvation by faith alone, holds the same position.

The Mahābhārata poem says: "Like fishes going against a current of water, the acts of a past life are flung back on the actor." There are some schools of Hinduism which allow for grace to set aside the punishment of evil deeds. But even they do not logically teach that a man by his own good deeds can remove the evil of his wrong deeds. In this too the Hindu doctrine resembles the Christian, which teaches that, even if a man had never committed a sin, his having lived righteously would not bring him a salvation earned by his good deeds, for by living a good life he had simply done his duty and no more. A fourth excellence in the Karmic doctrine is its emphasis on *personal* punishment, because every one must *himself* reap the fruit of every one of his deeds. A Hindu book says: "As amongst a thousand cows a calf knows its mother, so the deed done before finds out its doer." While this is plainly the intention, the imperfections of the doctrine in actual life work out a different result, viz.: since the sorrows and trials of this life are deemed by Karma an expiation not of deeds done in this life, of which one can be conscious, but are wholly the fruit of unknown evil deeds in an unremembered past, and since any sins in this present life are not to be expiated here, but wholly in some unknown future, the sense of guilt and of punishment for sin must be very light. Here again are arrest and degeneracy.

While we should recognize such advantages in the Karma doctrine, we need also to give attention to its very serious defects. The first significant fact is that the highest Hinduism itself practically criticises and expresses dissatisfaction with the Karma system. This comes from a doctrine which always accompanies the Karmic doctrine, viz.: the desire and the way of escape from Karma. If the Karma system were entirely satisfactory morally, why should Release from an entirely satisfactory system be desired? Yet every Hindu desires and hopes to be released from that system. This shows that, at bottom, both the Hindu heart and mind are not satisfied with the outcome of the Karma idea. If the Karma system were morally satisfactory, it would not be moral to desire to escape from it. The consistent pantheism of the thoroughgoing Vedanta school is logically a clear expression of the unsatisfactoriness of the Karma system as a whole, for, according to pure pantheism, a man can be deemed to have reached his goal only when he has risen into a state in which morality and consciousness are transcended.

The assumption of the Karmic doctrine is that every man's condition in this state of existence is exactly the fruit of his deeds in a previous unremembered soul-embodiment. The first criticism on this position is that, of necessity, it is and can be, only an unprovable hypothesis. For, though occasionally a man may claim that he remembers some of the experience of a previous existence, manifestly that claim cannot be tested whether it is true or not. The law of Karma also conceives that there must be an absolute proportion between the heinousness of an evil deed and the unpleasantness of its fruit in the next state of existence. But the appeal to life, which must be the last test of everything, shows that in the realm of human experience this is not true. New influences are constantly coming in to disturb the exact relation between the cause and the effect of any single deed. This uncertainty as to what additional and disturbing elements may have come in to modify the effect of actions is a fact of every-day life which distinctly denies the basal assumption of the law of Karma. The theory of evolution, which is accepted by all modern science, recognizes the universal principle that while a favourable environment promotes the development of a certain species, an unfavourable environment extinguishes that species. The same law applies to moral causes and effects. The law of Karma contravenes this well-known law.

This defect in the Karma doctrine is one main cause of the Hindu's lack of interest in history. To the believer in Karma history can have no interest or significance, because it is merely a predetermined, unavoidable sequence of events. To us, history is full of moral stimulus, because it shows how one man can affect, for good or evil, the destinies of other men and even nations. Though to a limited degree the Karma doctrine allows that a man can influence the lives of others, yet he cannot really influence the destiny of a single individual. That destiny is unalterably fixed for each individual by his Karma in a previous stage of existence. All that one can do for another in this world is to provide a means by which that other's previously determined condition may be fulfilled. He can help others only because, in a previous existence, they so acted as to receive in this life, from him or from others, the help which they may thus receive. If a man harms others, it is only because in a previous existence they acted so as to receive this harm from him or from some one. But the experience of life shows the unsoundness of this assumption in the Karma doctrine, because the consequences of both good and evil actions are more or less being avoided every day. "If human wisdom can counteract and, by transforming, can nullify the natural evil consequences of many deeds, much more may the divine purpose, which is working itself out in the evolution of the universe, make for righteousness and forgiveness, in spite of evil deeds of men of which the natural consequence would be universal ruin." While the law of Karma strictly teaches that there can be no deviation from inevitable results, there are some schools of Hindu thought which teach that, under some circumstances, the gods can modify the consequences of actions.

Still another defect in the Karma doctrine when logically accepted is that the entire purpose of the present order is judicial, and not one for the education and formation of character: the only object and purpose of the present is the requital of the past. As a response to conscience, the doctrine of transmigration had a real moral value, because it recognized the need that, since full reward and punishment of good and evil does not appear in the present life, this should and will be meted out in the next stage of existence. So, despite the fatalistic implications in the doctrine that one's condition in this life is the equivalent of one's previous life, it did imply that the divine powers see that human goodness and badness get their merited deserts. This gave importance to living right in the present world.

But the fully developed transmigration doctrine makes the present world to have only judicial significance, for not only is the future to be a requital of the present, but the present is merely a requital of one's actions in a past existence. However, there can be no inspiration in life, if the only meaning and purpose of this life are simply to expiate a past unremembered life. In the Christian view, man's object in life is to fit himself into the high purpose of the one Father of all men, who is ever trying to make the most of every human being, and is helping him to do his part. But in the Karma system there is no universal purpose except the judicial one of requital for the past. According to that system, justice for the sake of justice is " like an attribute with no substance in which to adhere; judgment for the sake of judgment is like a prison system without any State."

When the Hindu mind, in its effort to attain intellectual consistency, developed these thorough-going doctrines of Karma and transmigration and release therefrom by absorption into the unconscious Brahma, I believe that it was God Himself who showed the Hindu the inadequacy of his metaphysic. The heart of the Hindu protested against the doctrine that the only end of existence in this world is the judicial one of requiring the soul to consume the fruits of its action in a previous existence. The heart of the Hindu, like the heart of men everywhere, believes that beyond this life there is something truly good, and that we can so live in this world as to attain that future infinite good. Under God it was this deep conviction of the human soul which led the Hindu to be dissatisfied with the law of Karma, which, if unmodified, would have made endless re-births and endless existence the necessary unavoidable fate of every one. So the doctrine of Release from the working of Karma through knowledge and thereby through absorption into the only Reality, led the Hindu to accept, and to find satisfaction in the doctrine of absorption, because it seemed better than the Karmic doctrine of endless re-births and re-deaths.

For the same reason some men now commit suicide, blindly assuming that escape from what appears unbearable evil and hoped-for cessation of existence are better than the painful experiences of their present lives. In doctrine, as in life, suicide is confession. The fact that the Hindu thinker preferred eternal suicide to the eternal working of the Karmic system is proof positive that that doctrine did not satisfy his heart nor his intellect. So the Hindu himself declares the basal doctrine of Hinduism to be unsatisfactory. Because this release from the hopelessness of the Karma doctrine was a desirable change, I believe that even the unsatisfying transmigration doctrine was the Hindu thinker's response to a suggestion from God; though an entirely satisfying response will only come when the Hindu accepts as the master of his thought and life One who has brought life and immortality to light through His gospel.

As stated above, one advantage of the Karma doctrine is that it offers a plausible solution of the problem why there appear so many undeserved inequalities in the lot of men. By the Karma doctrine the explanation is clear, viz. this: a just god cannot dispense unmerited suffering, but the sufferings of men in this life do not correspond to the deserts of each; therefore, these sufferings must be proportioned to the acts and deserts of men in previous embodiments. Hindu satisfaction with the Karmic doctrine is mainly due to this apparently satisfactory solution. Had the Hindu known the experience and teaching of Christ that it is godlike to bear undeserved suffering in order to help and to save weak and erring fellow men, he might not for centuries have been content with the assumption that suffering unmerited trouble is an injustice and an evil, unless it is a requital for wrongdoing in a previous existence. God made the Hindu feel that the author of the universe could not be unjust; and so, groping after the unknown god, the Hindu thought out the doctrines of Karma and transmigration because he had not found any other explanation of the inequalities of life. So hard is it for men, even after long thought, to see God as He is, and to understand the mystery of suffering, when they are unaided by the revelation of God through a perfect human life, whose controlling passion was through unmerited suffering to win men to their heavenly Father.

The final defect of the Karma-transmigration doctrine is that consistency led the Hindu thinker to take an additional logical step, viz.: to consider the phenomenal world as entirely illusory and unreal. Both the mind and heart of the Hindu groping after God would not rest until it could believe that it had found ultimate reality. The Hindu explanation of the world on the Karma-transmigration theory did not satisfactorily explain the mystery of the universe. There seemed to the Hindu mind and heart an unreality in life. Therefore, the Hindu heart even more than the Hindu mind said for substance: "The world being unreal, leap into the only reality; leap into the absolute unknown, and thereby become absorbed into the great reality." I cannot help interpreting this leap as, at bottom, a response to the Spirit of God. The Karma doctrine is pessimistic. The doctrine of absorption into the ultimate reality was the optimistic wish to leap from unreality into reality. This longing is thus expressed in the Brihad Aranyaka Upanishad:

> "From the unreal lead me to the real.
> From darkness lead me to the light.
> From death lead me to immortality."

Yet here was another characteristic illustration of much of India's thought and life; a strange excess of inference. The pendulum swings to the opposite extreme. Here I stop with this analysis of the most fundamental and universal doctrine of India, but in the final lecture shall again refer to it in an attempt to show how this may be considered and used as a preparation for the Christ.

Hinduism is not only, and not mainly, a combination of religious doctrines and practices. It is also a social organization resting on the institution of caste, which is the universal and determinative feature of everyday Hinduism. So, in an interpretation of India's religious history, at least a brief analysis of this institution is needed. Though it is not uncommon to consider the caste system as wholly a device of the devil, it can be shown that, in this institution too, can be seen the hand of God. Few institutions which have very wide acceptance and long life in a large community are wholly bad. The assumption that God is ever seeking His human children and that they are ever groping after Him, though often in ignorance and sin, would indicate that such an institution was another illustration of the struggle of the spirit against the flesh and of the flesh against the spirit. And the greater the final victory of the flesh over the spirit, the greater the need of the Christ, and the reason for the expectation that when the Spirit of Christ transforms the institution, its better elements will be not destroyed, but fulfilled. In social institutions, as well as in religious thought and practice, the Christ lives not to destroy, but to fulfil.

That caste started from a natural ethnical basis is shown first from the original word for caste which means colour (*varna*); and secondly, from the early habit continued to the present, of considering the Aryans "twice born," and the non-Aryans only "once born."

While caste started with race distinction. a second and most influential cause of classification was occupation. The third main working principle was geographical location The devil had nothing to do with these powerful and controlling influences of ethnical, occupational, and geographical character, which originally determined the social status. As the Aryans spread through the land and more or less mingled with the aborigines, and as wars and the requirements of life caused manifold cross-divisions of location and occupation, complexity arose in the social organization, and innumerable divisions and subdivisions of castes easily arose. There are hundreds of subdivisions of the Brahman class, and thousands of divisions and subdivisions of other castes and outcasts. In many of these distinctions there is nothing blameworthy. They exist in every community on earth. And where the organization of society is quite complex, the distinctions are most numerous. Moreover, it is a part of the divine economy that many of these distinctions are, on the whole, helpful to society. Regarding, as we now do, society as an organism, is it not correct to say the social body is one, but hath many members; and God has set the members, each one in the body, according to ethnical, occupational, and geographical considerations, as it pleased Him; and if all were one member, where were the body? There are many members, but one body.

Yet, though Hindu caste started on this natural basis, it has, to a sad extent, shown that service and mutual helpfulness were too often not the controlling considerations of the favoured members, but pride of position and indifference or disregard of the less favoured. It is another illustration from India's history of the age-long universal struggle of the flesh against the spirit, in which the former, alas too often, wins the victory. Under the choking influence of the letter and the flesh, the mutual helpfulness, which was the beginning of the caste movement, has so bound its spirit that India now calls out: "Who shall deliver me from the bondage of this death?"

A little more detail about the formation and development of the caste system is as follows: In primitive Aryan Society, each father was the priest of his family. Gradually some men in the community became learned and wise in the conduct of religious rites and sacrifices. Such eminence became hereditary in families. The religious hymns and liturgies were not written, but were passed from generation to generation by oral teaching. The knowledge of such hymns and liturgies became a valuable property. The families which got a hereditary claim to conduct religious ceremonies and to interpret the hymns and liturgies naturally did all they could to make the ceremonies imposing. There grew up a hierarchy among all such ministrants. The most learned wrote out religious books. Then, as the ceremonies became more elaborate and the priests more numerous, the priestly class of Brahmans was formed. From their learning and from their connection with religion the Brahmans became the most influential and highest caste. No explanation is needed for the development of the next highest caste, that of kings and warriors; nor of the third caste, that of the farmers; nor of the fourth original caste, that of the servile community, called Sudras, who are mostly from the conquered aborgines. Yet this development was not by any means always peacefully effected. The exclusive claims of the Brahmans were often objected to, and sometimes were successfully resisted, by the warrior class, some of whose members were thoughtful and learned and pious. Also members of the third, or cultivator caste, doubtless sometimes aspired to and were received into the warrior caste. But the Brahmans have usually been shrewd, and by not aspiring to be kings, but the guides and counsellors of all, they have usually won obedience from all classes.

One of the proper influences which originally brought about the caste system was the desire and effort to maintain family and tribal purity. Modern society has not yet adequately learned how to prohibit and restrain undesirable intermarriages. The numerous wars and conquests of the Aryans constantly exposed them to illicit and undesirable sexual and marriage relations. In the effort to limit such evil, elaborate caste restrictions about marriage were formed and somewhat enforced. Another legitimate influence in developing caste was the economic consideration which developed trade-guilds in Europe and is causing trade-unions in most countries at this time. Caste regulations have crystallized in every occupation, and internally have done some good. Caste as a trade-union insists on and secures the proper training of the youth of the craft; it exerts much influence in regulating the wages of its members, deals with trade delinquents, promotes good fellowship and charity among its members, by public opinion and penalties in a general way it keeps the standard of thought and life at a moderate level, all enforced by public opinion and caste rule. For keeping society at a moderate level and preventing social decay, there has never been developed a force like caste. So far, so good.

But the good is not only the worst enemy of the best, it tends to decay. So has it been with the caste system in India. Even at its best it could only keep society at a dead level. However, it not only prevented its members from slipping down, but also from rising. Past custom became not only controlling, but tyrannical. In no social system have individual initiative and motive for aspiration and opportunity for new attainments been so absolutely and so ruthlessly repressed. One-caste of the population of India to-day are by caste classified as "untouchables." According to strict caste rules not only the touch, but the shadow, of any one of these millions causes pollution. Such a result has crushed hope and self-respect out of this immense section of the body politic, not only to their own injury, but also to the impoverishment of the entire community.

While this injury has come to the depressed classes, the caste system has wrought, perhaps, even greater injury to the high castes. It has made them proud, haughty, unsympathetic, and unprogressive. According to caste, a man is polluted by going from India to a foreign country for an education. This excessive restriction has done countless harm to India's progress. Originally intended only to guard purity in the forming of marriage alliances, it has needlessly hedged marriage about with harassing restrictions. Originally intended to help religion and to assure that religious service shall be regularly and properly carried on, caste has become a most tyrannical and repressive organization, choking the spirit of religion. To-day the majority of even intelligent people dare not follow their consciences by refraining from religious practices which they despise, or by publicly expressing their true beliefs. Those who are not Indians can have slight knowledge of the tremendous annoyance and injury which intelligent men and women suffer from the caste system as it now exists. The best Indians are themselves constantly bewailing the injury which this social organization is doing to them and to their country.

This analysis of the origin, the advantages and disadvantages of the caste system has, I hope, been an interpretation of how the spirit and the flesh have struggled in India, and how, alas! lower considerations have often won the victory over higher ones. "Caste is the arrested attempt at the organization of society on lines which, at the beginning, recognized the organic unity of society as a whole." At first it implied and required the reciprocal helpfulness of all its parts. It started with recognition of the fact that every part of society should consider itself intended for, and bound to help every other part, and that each could best serve even itself by unselfishly serving every other part. But no social system ever so thoroughly lost recognition of the principle of *noblesse oblige.* The upper classes misunderstood and misapplied the only legitimate basis of privilege, viz.: the larger opportunity and larger obligation of glad and unselfish helpfulness to others. Then, of course, all society was debased.

Perhaps the upper castes have, on the whole, been the worst sufferers, because, by their interpretation of the reasons of caste distinctions, they have assumed that the lower castes existed only for the good of the upper, instead of the reverse. This has made them, as a rule, selfish, proud, and inconsiderate. Caste was originally organized to be, and to a certain extent has been, a means of giving individuals the guidance and strength of custom in doing what was deemed right, which, without such guidance and aid, individuals would not so uniformly do. But when caste reversed its only legitimate basis that glad service is the natural crown of special privilege, it lost its meaning and value. In India it has become tyranny. In religion it has promoted formalism, hypocrisy, and pride. In society it has been the chief cause of arrest in progress and in mutual helpfulness. In contact with Christian principles and modern ideas, it is rapidly disintegrating, but under the influence of the Christ, the basal idea of this social organization can be, and I believe, is to be fulfilled.

IV

THE GREATNESS AND WEAKNESS OF HINDUISM

IN religion, as in physical nature, the persistence of any phase of life is indubitable evidence that there was some need of that development and that it possessed inherent force. For at least five thousand years the varying phases of Hinduism have expressed and have given some measure of satisfaction to the religious needs of an immense number of human beings. That is evidence enough that such a system had elements of worth and power. On the assumption underlying these lectures that God has never left any community without witness of Himself, and that the divine Spirit, on account of His gracious and universal character, must ever be at least attempting to guide and teach men, we should expect to find in the Hindu religion elements of power. On the other hand, the history of the religious thought and light, even of peoples who call themselves Christian, shows how sadly persistent and forceful has been the struggle of lower against higher considerations. Still more should we expect to find elements of great weakness in a religion like Hinduism, which has not had the privilege of a revelation of the Christ. The present lecture is an attempt to point out some of the greatness and some of the weakness of the higher Hinduism.*

It is needless to show that popular Hinduism is doomed. Its features are superstition, degrading ceremonialism, polytheism, idolatry, and all the undesirable characteristics of caste. One clear, indubitable evidence that the divine Spirit has not been inactive in India is that for centuries many earnest Indians have protested against those bad characteristics of popular Hinduism; and that sometimes the protests have resulted in considerable reforms for a considerable time. Nowadays also, many spiritual-minded and earnest non-Christians, as well as Christians,

* In this lecture great obligation is acknowledged to Articles in the *Contemporary Review* by J. N. Farquhar, M.A.

are working hard to lead the followers of popular Hinduism to leave it for purer thought and better ways. All agree that popular Hinduism is doomed. But, thereby, the higher Hinduism is being released from some of its incumbrances, and its excellences are being better known and more appreciated in the West, as well as in the East. Therefore, it is necessary and fair to look into both the greatness and the weakness of this higher Hinduism. If its best features are the work of the divine Spirit, then to the believer in the Christ those features should certainly be an encouragement. Every true element in any religion is something which the Christ came not to destroy, but to fulfil.

Hinduism, as a whole, has many elements of power: elements tending to bring that religion to the highest grade, yet never reaching that grade because those good features are connected with some fatal elements of weakness. The first mark of greatness in the higher Hinduism is the acuteness and consistency of its thought. Probably no religion in the world equals Hinduism in intellectual keenness. Notice that I do not say that Hindu thought excels in correctness, but only that it excels in keenness and in consistency from assumed premisses. In intellectual vigour, Hinduism is a great religion. For millenniums it has had thinkers who have patiently, insistently meditated on the basal questions of ontology, on the spirit, on the problem of evil, on the highest good, and how to attain to this. And while they differed among themselves, yet in the main, they have thought these profound questions through till they have come to consistent conclusions. Had their presuppositions been correct, they would have come to a better conclusion. Despite differences of assumption and of intermediate inferences, there has been a remarkable thoroughness and consistency in their final conclusions. Practically all Hindu schools believe in a monistic philosophy. The West is late in a growing tendency to the same general position.

Two assumptions about the phenomenal universe and about ultimate reality underlie all Hindu thought. The first assumption is that the world exists solely that the soul may consume the fruit of its actions in a previous stage of existence. If true, this hypothesis would give a system of strict justice, bringing to every one reward and punishment in exact measure for the good or evil done by him aforetime. Also, if this were true, then consistently the world-process must be, as Hindu thought asserts, eternal, for otherwise there would be no explanation of its beginning and no justification for ending it. The second assumption is that only the divine is real, and that everything phenomenal is unreal. Both assumptions are due to long meditation on the mysteries of life with the desire to think through to simple, ultimate truth. Granted the two premisses, that the world-process is solely retributive and that the only reality is that which is behind the apparent, the Hindu conclusion logically follows, viz.: the one who knows the truth should seek escape from the sorrow and unreality of the world by absorption into the real. Some thinkers in the West also have drawn this same conclusion, whose life has not been spent in sturdy hand-to-hand grapple with the troubles of the world, and who have not found in the Christ the way, the truth, and the life, but, like Hindu thinkers, have imagined that full-orbed truth about fundamentals can be secured by lonely meditation.

The first Hindu assumption is a great conception, for it fully recognizes the immensity of the unmerited sorrows and inequalities of the world, yet holds to the inevitable connection of cause and effect in the moral, as in the physical world, and, without a knowledge of a personal and loving God, it finds the only logical solution in an endless and just retributive world-process. The second assumption also is a great conception, for it recognizes, that despite the perplexity and seeming unreality of visible and experienced processes, there is a great reality underlying the universe. And despite the natural pessimism of the second assumption, there is an underlying optimism in the conclusion from the two premisses, viz.: that it is possible to escape from the unreal to the real, and also an underlying courage in the determination, and effort, at all costs, to effect that escape.

The thorough-going qualities of these two

assumptions and of their conclusions, account for a great many strange accompaniments of Hinduism. The assumed unreality of the world has easily condoned and even encouraged belief in innumerable deities who are not themselves the ultimate reality, but who may be the means of communicating with the Incommunicable. For the same reason this philosophy allows idols to the unenlightened. Also the unreality of the world teaches that the human body has no value and should be subjected to asceticism. Ordered society is a delusive attempt to make men satisfied with an existence which should rather be made uncomfortable. Religious ceremonies are an idle and even a selfish search for vain blessing from unreal gods. Knowledge is the only thing to be desired, for only by knowledge that the world is unreal and that what is behind the phenomenal is the real, can one escape from transmigration, and from the ocean of vain sense impressions to the bliss of absorption into the ultimate Reality. The clear evidence that this thorough-going and large conception has had great power in weaning men from what seemed low into strenuous sacrifice for the highest is seen in the completeness and eagerness with which countless Hindu ascetics have subjected their bodies to nameless torture in their sincere efforts to attain the highest end of life.

While intellectual acuteness is one mark of greatness in the higher Hinduism, an intensity of reverence for the Spirit constitutes another element of its greatness. Notice that I call this a mark of the greatness of Hinduism, though I do not call it complete or satisfactory. Every Hindu considers the Spirit supreme. It is one of the anomalies of Hinduism that, while an excess of endless ceremonies, most of which probably have little clear significance to the worshipper or even to the officiating priest, constitutes the main part of the average Hindu's outward religion, yet even the degraded and superstitious followers of popular Hinduism somehow believe that there is a great Spirit behind and beyond every form. The very structure of the ordinary idol-temple is of a kind to awaken a suggestion of the vague unknown. The power of all Hinduism seems to me to lie in creating a sense of the vague, infinite unknown, which, being invisible, must be spirit. And to the higher Hinduism the Spirit is the sole reality. The imagination is probably the most active and extraordinarily developed mental power of the Hindu, and everywhere the imagination revels in the invisible. It was this power which gave development to pantheism. The first type of monistic philosophy of India was not an impersonal monism, but an incipient monotheism. Before the Vedantic type of pantheism was elaborated, the Indian thinker posited the Atman, the spirit, and the Paramātman, the great Spirit.

Also, after the Vedantic pantheism became prevalent, there arose eminent thinkers, as well as earnest reformers, who developed a modified philosophy called the Dvaita or the Vishisth-advaita Vedanta, which insisted on a personal character in every divinity. This qualified monism was not as consistently logical a system as pure pantheism, but it was the expression of true thought and yearning, and the leaders in such movements are among the greatest theistic saints of Hindustan. Leaders like Rāmānuja and Rāmānanda developed the type of Hinduism which passes under the general name of Vaishnavism, which expresses religion under more human and personal aspects than most schools of Indian thought. It is Vaishnavism which has developed the doctrine of incarnation, and the better phases of those incarnations have been human incarnations. Buddhism and Jainism, while less spiritual, were also protests against ceremonialism, the sacrificial system, and cold pantheism, and were systems of a more spiritual faith and ethical life. Above all the most influential poets of India have been men of an intensely spiritual bent, many of whom poured contempt on a materialistic and formal conception of religion, and emphasized the spirit, even when their popular divinities had many unworthy attributes. Later reformers, like Nānak and Kabir, were men who magnified the spirit. The influence of the Bhagavad Gita, which is the most influential religious book of India, is spiritual. Those Christians do not deal fairly with Hinduism who decry the alleged immoralities of the Krishna of the later Purānās, and fail to respect the Krishna who is the spiritual hero of the Divine Song.

At bottom, asceticism also is a real, though mistaken, emphasis on the supremacy of the spirit, and no religion has developed asceticism like Hinduism. Also though Hinduism teaches that the way of knowledge (the *jnanmārga*) is the highest way of reaching the divine, and that the way of works (the *karmamārga*) is the lowest way, it teaches that there is another and a noble way of salvation, viz.: the way of loving devotion or faith (the *bhaktimārga*). This last is an approximation to the Christian doctrine of salvation by faith. Among some Christian churches the doctrine of salvation by faith has sometimes come almost to mean salvation by so-called orthodox thinking, which is the Western counterpart of what the Hindus call their highest way, that of salvation by knowledge. In some phases of the higher Hinduism there is greatness in the intensity of the search after the spirit.

A third element of greatness in Hinduism is in its organization. Organization is, or at least should be, to religion, what the body is to the soul, a means of expressing and giving opportunity to the spirit. Instead of being a servant of the spirit, the human body has often become its master, and instead of expressing has depressed the spirit. Similarly, in every religion, the outward organization has often debased and choked the spirit. Nevertheless, as a sound spirit requires and develops a sound body, so every religion requires a vigorous organization. And a vigorous organization indicates power in the religion which first developed it, even though later that organization may have enslaved the spirit.

Hinduism has one mark of greatness in an exceptionally effective organization. Notice that I do not call it a satisfactory, but a great, organization. The organization of Hinduism is the most thorough-going and effective religious organization in the world. It consists of the universal acceptance of three elements which are found in any all-powerful religious organization, viz.: first, an authoritative and accepted book or standard; second, an authoritative and influential body of interpreters and administrators of the recognized standard; and third, a powerful public sentiment, which uniformly yields obedience to the standard and to its interpreters, and which is crystallized in a social system. Hinduism has these three elements in the highest measure.

First, all Hindus consider the Vedas, i.e. their oldest religious books, as inspired and authoritative. So complete is the claim for their inspiration, that the priests assert that the Vedas were direct utterances from the mouth of God, even without being written; and for ages they were not written, but were passed from generation to generation by oral repetition. Even Hindu philosophers, whose belief and teaching absolutely disregard the plain meaning of the Vedas, have always *professed* to draw their doctrine from those books, and to hold them as the highest authority. So great is the superstitious reverence for those books, the evident meaning of which only began to be made clear by Western scholars less than a century ago, that today in Benares, the most sacred city of Hinduism, Brahmans, who are fairly intelligent on many things, actually believe that these simple, ancient writings contain accounts and predictions of all modern science and discovery, that they show that the Vedic writers knew of ocean steamships, the telegraph, automobiles, airships, etc. The organization of Hinduism begins with the power of sacred writings, so revered and so absolutely authoritative.

Secondly, in the Brahmans Hinduism has a body of strong, determined men, who are universally recognized as the authoritative interpreters and administrators of the religion. So great has this power of the Brahman been esteemed that his anger or his curse was dreaded far more than any other possible evil.

Thirdly, in caste Hinduism has had for its organization the most powerful social system which the world has ever seen, with practically entire public sentiment supporting it. Despite the restlessness of the nobler spirits who have denounced caste, despite its vicissitudes in the Buddhist revolt and temporary ascendency, it has for thousands of years been, and still is, the chief power of Hinduism. For the most part, the Brahmans have been the thinkers of Hinduism. In considerable part, they have been the makers of a great literature. But their chief achievement has been their gradually, yet universally, bringing the entire religious and social system of many races, with many religious types and degrees of culture, under loyal subservience to themselves. And the caste system, which has arisen in various ways, has been the principal cause of the cohesion and power of Hinduism.

A fourth element of greatness in Hinduism has been the compass and variety of its appeal to the religious nature. Hinduism makes an appeal to every side of man. As shown above, it is strong in its intellectual and spiritual appeal, and its appeal to the instinct of most men who crave direction by an authority which believes in itself as to what is true and right and what must be done. In addition, Hinduism is rich in its provision for stimulating the craving for worship. Any unusual event in any place, any striking object in nature, any auspicious or fearful natural force has made that place a holy place, that object or that force an object or force worthy of worship. As in ancient Israel, so in Hindustan, on every high hill and under every green tree, there is an idol or some sacred object and a place of pilgrimage. Since the eye is the principal gateway to the mind, Hinduism provides, through idols and other visible objects, stimulus to worship. The spirit of worship is developed by extensive and costly temples, adorned with sculpture and fresco, illustrating religious myths, and with awe-inspiring, darkened interiors, into the mysterious recesses of which the ordinary man cannot go. At every gateway of every tiniest village is a temple containing an idol, which calls for some act of adoration from every one as he enters or departs from the village. On the borders of each village, and at many graves, there is some structure, humble or large, which suggests something to be feared or revered, while little shrines abound everywhere.

In early times sacrifices were a large part of religion, though nowadays they are more rare. The sacramental meal was an early and impressive element of common worship, and still continues in some places (e.g. at Puri, in Orissa, and at Pandharpur, in Western India). Praise, expressed by the singing of popular lyrics, often accompanied by simple instruments or at least by clapping of hands and movements of the body, is a worthy part of worship. In Hinduism, theoretically, no one should worship without presenting some gift, at least of flowers, to the god.

In addition to visits to public temples, shrines, and sacred places, for the devout man, there are daily rites, prayers, and offerings in the homes, annual festivals, and occasional ceremonies and feasts for births, stated periods of growth, sickness, death, and after death. These may be of a simple and inexpensive nature for the poor, or elaborate and costly for the rich. They all cultivate the religious nature. In no religion have mythology and hero worship been so abundant and influential as in Hinduism. When these stories are related or sung, their semi-religious narration holds great masses spell-bound. Such public recitals are the principal means by which the ideas of Hinduism are communicated to the masses. So in manifold ways, every element of life is made sacred and a means of developing the religious nature. Finally, all is enforced by the priestly class, which has a part in many of the minor and all the major acts of worship.

Since we are considering the greatness and weakness of India's religious life, as well as thought, I specify as one element of greatness in Hinduism, its power to promote the solidarity and stability of society. In a previous lecture I gave an analysis of caste. It certainly is a very strong institution and has done one great service to Indian society. It has given to the community a unitedness such as has not been secured elsewhere. It has made the community really believe that all men who are in the Hindu pale are inseparably linked, are responsible for each other, and must on no account and under no circumstances be parted from one another. "The practical result has been to give an intensity to the corporate life of the Hindu community which has never been exemplified elsewhere." This is a lower conception than the Christian doctrine of the brotherhood of men. For it is not the unitedness of every man with every other man as a brother, but somewhat like the unitedness of interest between the members of a trade union, whose outlook and interest are confined to the members of the group.

Another element of greatness in Hinduism is its conservative appreciation of the past. As the West grows maturer, it is slowly growing into appreciation of the fact that one supreme law of life is continuity; that, while looking forward for additional development, no form of life, no institution, no religion, can or will safely lose respect for its origins. One main element in the significance of history is the conviction of the solidarity of the social organism, that is, of the value of the past. The basis of the power of the six non-theological commandments of the Biblical decalogue is a recognition of the importance of a right attitude toward the past. It is this element which has constituted one main source of strength to such a system as Confucianism. This is one of the great elements of Hinduism. In thought and in practice, ideal Hinduism has had reverence for the past. This has brought it about that, in India, the fifth commandment of respect for elders is probably better obeyed than in America. Also the tenth commandment is unquestionably better obeyed by the Hindu than by the Anglo-Saxon. The Hindu is more content with his lot than the Westerner. He rarely covets.

I have tried to give a correct and fair estimate of some of the elements which have given the higher Hinduism a hold on from one-fifth to one-sixth of the human race for thousands of years. I have ascribed the inspiration of these best elements to God. But there are also many elements of weakness in even the higher, as well as in popular, Hinduism. In general, the weaknesses of Hinduism are the one-sided and excessive developments of its strong elements, without the balance of complementary truths. Thus the first element of strength described above, viz.: acuteness of thought, resulted in the fundamental weakness which characterizes most of the higher Hinduism, viz.: that of cold intellectualism. The thought of higher Hinduism has not been an appeal to life in all its aspects, but an appeal to logic. It shows the hopelessness of attempts at spiritual flight with only one wing. The acute thinkers who, in the attempt to reach a consistent ultimate unity for the universe, found it in an impersonal monism never satisfied the heart of Hinduism. Hinduism has never secured a satisfactory conception of God. By its wisdom Hinduism knew not a personal God and rested in an ultimate It, to whom no man can pray, whom no man can love, and in gratitude to whom no man can serve brother men.

By what it considered wisdom the higher Hinduism also knew not man, but counted him and all his experiences unreal, and his highest good to be absorption into the universal It. According to this cold intellectualism all religious acts and institutions are only a sham and a selfish courting of unreal divinities. Everything is unreal, is a mirage, is *māyā*. Hinduism has never had a satisfactory conception of man. When intelligent free moral agents with intellect, heart, and will, by an intellectual process come to affirm and to believe that they are not persons, but are unreal, and will become real only when they lose consciousness and are absorbed into an unthinking, universal It, the light of reason in them becomes darkness, and how great is that darkness.

The second element of strength, viz.: intensity of search after the Spirit, has been accompanied by an unregulated imagination. The Hindu can believe in the teeth of clear evidence, because the ideals of his imagination seem more conclusive than the evidences of the experience of life. An excess of imagination, like an excess of metaphysical consistency, vitiates sound conclusions. We see among some modern Christians the same kind of superstition which has been and still is, a weakness in Hindus, viz.: unwillingness and even fear of a careful and thorough historical examination of the origins of their faith, and hesitation in comparing these origins with the origins of other religions. The *bhakti* doctrine of salvation by loving devotion, which somewhat approaches the Christian doctrine, has often come to mean that faith by itself brings salvation, regardless of the one on whom faith is placed.

An excessively exuberant imagination has made the Hindu satisfied with a subjective conviction, regardless of the objective legitimacy or satisfactoriness of the ground of his faith and hope. Nor has Hinduism developed a clear and ethical conception that salvation is purely a matter of character.

The third element of greatness in Hinduism, viz.: an all-embracing and effective organization, has also proved a source of most marked weakness. Humble, unselfish, spiritual leadership is necessary and effective. But when leaders become proud, and selfish, and mechanical, then they debase themselves and debase their followers. They are blind leaders of the blind. Both fall into the ditch. This has come to be the condition of the Brahmans and of the Brahmanical ascendency in Hinduism.

A fourth weakness of Hinduism is its unethical character as a whole. An ultimate Reality, which is impersonal, must be unethical. Even when that Reality is conceived to have some personal nature, if the way of knowledge is the highest way, then the chief weakness in men is not sin, but ignorance. Neither the higher nor the lower Hinduism has any adequate conception of sin.

A fifth weakness of the higher Hinduism is its necessary lack of altruism. Where the goal is knowledge for one's self, in order that the self may attain its goal of absorption, there is no stimulus to serve others. Those others really do not need service. They *must* themselves consume the fruit of their deeds in a previous existence. No aid from other men can interfere with that. Nor is there any motive to serve society. The world being unreal, escape from it and from all men is the ideal for the enlightened man.

A sixth weakness is the inaction, the unprogressiveness, the dull contentment with things as they are, which result from the conception of the world as unreal, and from the Karma doctrine that every man must inevitably be what he is.

Again, at this stage of the world it is a fatal weakness that any institution or any idea should be contracted in scope and applicability. Hinduism is, and can be, only a national religion. No one can be a Hindu except one who is born such. Intellectually he may accept the doctrines of Hinduism, but he can never become a true Hindu. Even in the past every national religion, which came into contact with the Christian religion, unavoidably passed away. The fact that it was a national religion was one sufficient reason why it faded before a universal religion like the Christian. Where to-day are the religions of Egypt, Babylonia, Greece, Rome, and Scandinavia? The same reasons which caused their decline are undermining Hinduism to-day. Of these reasons one is that, by its essential principle, Hinduism is contracted and selfish and unavailable for those outside of its pale. It is not, and cannot be, a missionary faith. Universal applicability is essential now for any religion to satisfy thinking men anywhere.

This leads to the last mention of weakness in Hinduism, which will be dealt with in this connection. It is an absolutely fatal defect which dooms the system. Hinduism cannot cope with the modern spirit, i.e. it cannot meet the disintegrating influences of modern thought and life. India is being unavoidably modernized. This is manifesting itself in two marked tendencies. The first tendency is a new national spirit which expresses a new valuation of, and a new passion for, everything Indian. This new national spirit is active in political, social, and commercial matters, and naturally is active in religion also. There is a new pride in India's past, and a fresh confidence in her present and future. This national spirit leads many Indians to a new study of Hindu thought and philosophy, and to a Neo-Hinduism, which seeks to cast out the worst elements of popular Hinduism and to invigorate the best elements of the higher Hinduism.

But the leaven which is causing this ferment is India's contact with the West. Contact with the West means coming under the controlling element of modern life, the scientific spirit, which tests everything by its qualities of reality and of usefulness. It is contact with the West which is awakening the national spirit in political matters, in education, in social changes, in commercialism. That same leaven is the fermenting, assimilating power in the new interest in the Hindu religion and the confidence that, when purified, the Neo-Hindu faith will be sufficient for India. But the scientific spirit is utterly contradictory to the fundamental basis of Hinduism, which is that of the absolute authority of the standards of the past.

The contact of India with the modern spirit shows itself in two ways. First, because many doctrines and practices of Hinduism are seen not to be useful now, these worst elements are being discarded by the scientific spirit. Secondly, the scientific spirit is also radically undermining entire Hinduism by destroying confidence in the absolute authority of the past, for even its better elements. Whatever religion is to abide in India must be one which commends itself by its reality and by its usefulness to all classes of men in India and in the world. But, by cutting way the validity and sufficiency of any religious books and of any body of authorized interpreters, the scientific spirit which is now leavening India is eliminating Hinduism from remaining a religion which will continue to satisfy the thinking and spiritual men of that country. For Hinduism, as a system, the authority of the past has been the foundation. Neo-Hinduism of every shade practically discards this old foundation and appeals to modern Indians on the basis that what it would retain commends itself to the reason and religious nature of Indians. The more conservative schools of modern Hinduism do not discard the principle of excessive accommodation, which has always been characteristic of Hinduism. They may give up some portion of the worst superstitions, but when they do so, they apologize for the unethical and unspiritual concessions which they make to the masses. But apologies are always confessions. These very Neo-Hindus give the clearest testimony to the working of the modern scientific spirit by the apologies which they make for polytheism, idolatry, sacrifice, superstitious rites, and caste as unavoidable concessions to the masses.

The modern spirit discredits and undermines Hinduism in another of its fundamental positions. According to Hinduism, the world is unreal. On this assumption, Hinduism correctly teaches that the rôle for the wise and holy man is to escape from the world and engage in asceticism and meditation. But under the influence of the modern spirit the Indian heartily believes in the decided reality of the world, and more and more his thought and his action are all based on this conviction. This being so, instead of abjuring the world and devoting themselves to asceticism or meditation, most Indians are devoting themselves to the highest activity in the world, and the best men are devoting themselves to the betterment of society in business, politics, education, social improvement, and in religious enlightenment. But, whether they know it or not, by so doing these Indians are drifting away from the bases of Hinduism.

The doctrine of Karma is the most fundamental of Hindu doctrines. Its practical weakness is shown by its dissipation through contact with the modern spirit. The doctrine of Karma is, that every man's condition in the world is unalterably determined by his conduct in a previous stage of existence. Neither he nor any one else can alter his fate. Everything in the phenomenal world is the unchangeable result of previous Karma.

Karma settled it that the depressed classes are re-embodied souls which in previous stages of existence had done some evil on account of which they had re-birth in their present depressed condition, and in it they must irrevocably remain. But the logic of life is daily showing this assumption to be untrue. For, through the service of Christian missionaries, multitudes of those depressed classes are being marvellously raised. Also social reformers, political leaders, and earnest theists see that it is an economic, political, and religious wrong, both to the depressed classes and to the whole community, to let such a condition continue. So these Hindu leaders are making worthy efforts to elevate their depressed countrymen. Yet thereby they show their practical disbelief in two fundamentals of Hinduism, the religious doctrine of Karma and the social basis of caste. Before the vitalizing, energizing modern spirit, the Hindu theory of the world, the Karma doctrine, and the tyranny of caste are being disregarded, and will eventually be discarded entirely.

The inadequacy of Hindu doctrine and

Hindu caste is also illustrated by changes of sentiment and experience toward the highest castes. Once the anger and curse of a Brahman were deemed far more terrible than the anger of the gods or other punishment for sin. In India's dramatic literature, like the drama of Shakuntala, tragedy largely turned on the inevitable injury of a Brahman's imprecation. To-day, in many relations, the Brahman not only has no advantage, but is coming to be handicapped, and sometimes even despised. In the main, his respect depends more and more on his worth than on his birth. As an illustration, take an article from an influential Indian paper, *The Mysore and South Indian Review,* entitled: "The Brahmans; Should They Exist?" The first sentence of that article is this: "It is well known that the Brahmans are as much despised now as they were once held in high esteem." Other sentences in that article are these: The true Brahman "is one who is such, not only by birth, but by character and conduct, as well as in knowledge." "Not one in a thousand can at the present moment have a rightful and honest claim to that revered and high appellation." "The Brahmanism of the present day is, in fact, no Brahmanism at all. . . . it is a thing of the past." "The self-sacrifice of the Brahman of the good old days to get knowledge for its own sake is now entirely unknown." "The Brahman has prostituted knowledge for earning a living, and thus has debased it and at the same time lowered himself."

In short, the modern spirit is certainly and relentlessly undermining and disintegrating the assumptions and institutions of Hinduism by requiring every tradition, every custom, every doctrine, to approve itself as rational and useful. Formerly the sufficient condemnation of changes proposed by Christian missionaries or by the modern spirit was simply to say that the changes were contrary to, and subversive of, traditional authority. On that assumption it was unnecessary to show that many Hindu ideas and customs were injurious. Such evidence was irrelevant and inadmissible. The sanction of ancient religious books and of their interpretation by the Brahmans required unalterable compliance with old ideas and customs. Till recently so patent an advantage as visits by Indians to foreign countries for education and observation were prohibited by the Hindu religion. Child-marriages and the prohibition of the remarriage of even child widows were defended on the sufficient sanction of the shastras and custom. Those days are rapidly passing. Both the condemnation and defence of religious or social ideas and practices now come from the appeal to reason.

It is needless to give additional illustrations of the weakness of Hinduism. It is enough that it cannot meet the requirements of the modern spirit. Hinduism is doomed. Yet it has some worthy elements. God's way of dealing with men and with institutions and religions is not to destroy, but to fulfil. As unworthy elements in men, or in institutions, or religions pass away, if their best elements are fulfilled by a new environment, by complementary enlargements, by a new dynamic, then they pass into that which God intends. Thus we co-operate with God in His divine constructive way. The next lecture will be an attempt to show how, in the providence of God, Christ is the new dynamic; how the Spirit of Christ is to furnish the new environment; how God has prepared India for the Christ and Christ for India's development and highest usefulness to the world. In the past every gain in every department of life has been found to be simply a discovery by men of some wondrous thought and activity of God which had awaited recognition and utilization. To-day in every other department of life the lure to effort is the conviction that still more marvellous revelations of God's work await the reverent, patient investigator. Not less in Missions does a similar inspiring hope encourage to mightier effort the Christian man of insight. Therefore, enlarging the scope of Carey's great words to include the past as well as the future, the modern missionary should say: "Now seeing as never before God's great preparation in the past for India's becoming a reverent, obedient, loving disciple of the Christ, expect great things from God, attempt great things for God."

V

INDIA'S PREPARATION FOR THE CHRIST, AND CHRIST'S POWER TO MEET THAT PREPARATION

SO far as the preceding four lectures may have carried conviction, they have left the following distinct impressions: God has ever been at work in India; the Hindu has patiently sought after God; this long search has constantly met arrest and degeneracy; the moment that India came into contact with the Christ a marvellous change began in her thought and life; the higher Hinduism is passing away; therefore something must take its place. The present lecture is an attempt to show that the Christ can, and will, fulfil the best elements of Hinduism.

To any one who profoundly believes in God, India's marvellous, pathetic past is full of meaning and hope for the future. No handful of soil which is washed down from the eternal mountains, but helps to fertilize the plains where men congregate and toil. In the attrition of the modern spirit with both the lower and higher Hinduism, as the forms of the Indian religion are gradually rubbed and swept away, the better elements of both will enrich India's religious thought and life, and while doing this, under the germinating influence of the divine Spirit, will give a spiritual harvest for the life of the world. God has ever had His long look forward. The more patiently that He has waited, the more earnestly that for millenniums India has groped after God, the more certain the assurance that the fruitage of this divine patience will be large.

"God moves in a mysterious way His wonders to perform."
"Judge not the Lord by feeble sense, but trust Him for His grace."
"God is His own interpreter, and He will make it plain."

The more that one realizes that God has

been working for India, the more strong will be his conviction that the results of God's long, patient effort will be worthy of Himself. On such conviction every Christian child of the universal Father will be the more inspired to be a co-worker with God, on the Pauline principle: Work your best, because it is God that worketh for and through you. Using Christ's significant parable: He and His Spirit are a leaven which will leaven human thought and life till it is all leavened. The flour, the materials, of the parable are the thoughts and practices of any people. Christ and His Spirit are a leaven, a dynamic, which will influence the thought and life of the peoples with whom He comes into contact, and which He will gradually more and more influence, till they eventually all become Christlike. In this way the old ideas will have fuller and better significance and power, and will provide more nourishing bread for the souls of men.

It is unquestionably safe to say that, as yet, the thoughts and customs of not one man, not one community, not one church, have been wholly leavened by the Spirit of Christ. The leavening process has been only partially effected. In some individuals and some churches, more leavening has been accomplished than in others. Or, changing the figure and using another significant parable, in some of the better fields of the human heart or community, the good seed of Christ and His divine spirit may be yielding fruit, twenty-fold, thirty-fold, or possibly sixty-fold, —how much only He who seeth in secret truly knows,—but in not one is there already a hundred-fold fruitage. Also in some places the tares are choking the good seed more, and in others less. Nevertheless the good seed is growing; the tares are being more or less uprooted.

Also, before considering in detail the meaning of India's past for her future, it is desirable briefly to recall from the history of some other religions how the contact of the Christ with the thought and life of other countries prepared those peoples for the Christ and how He utilized their best heritage. Until to-day every religion that has come into contact with the Christ has sooner or later passed away, but from its own best thought and life it has always left an enriching element in the religious life which succeeded it. Is there not every reason to anticipate that there will be the same result in India's contact with the Christ? Those religions which passed away accomplished something worthy. They were in all cases a preparation for the Christ, who fulfilled every one of their elements. Not one jot or tittle of their law passed away without being fulfilled. It will be the same with Hinduism.

That which is called Christianity to-day practically consists of the thoughts and practices of the peoples to whom the church went, mixed with the ideas and modified by the inspiration which the church brought to those peoples. It is an axiom that the Hebrew religion made large contribution to what is called the Christian religion. This is the meaning of the Epistle to the Hebrews. This was the assumption and teaching of Paul. The Jewish religion was a scaffolding which was necessary and useful for the erection of the larger spiritual thought and life which

Christ introduced. But when the Christ was fully manifest, the Jewish preparation for Him had accomplished its work, and the scaffolding was ready to be taken down. The Hebrew religion contributed to the spiritual thought and life of the world its best element, viz.: conviction that God is a living and a righteous God. But, because at the time of the Christ the Hebrew leaders claimed that God was such a God mainly for His chosen people for their sakes, and not for the whole family of man, Judaism remained a contracted and national religion, which has never been thoroughly leavened by the universal Christ. The Greek contributed to the world an appreciation of beauty, but without the complementary truth of a strong ethical quality. So Greek civilization largely turned to voluptuousness, and therefore had to pass away. But both the Greek conception of beauty and the Greek philosophy have always been considered preparations for Christian thought and institutions, and have made them fuller. The Roman's chief contribution to the world has been a sense of law, order, and organization.

But, because the Roman had no adequate sense of responsibility for service, his thought and institutions hardened into tyranny, and therefore had to pass away. However, that Roman conception was a preparation for the Christ, who took and measurably fulfilled it, though again in so-called Christianity that organizing element has often tended to be tyrannical. To the thought and life of the Western world the Teutons contributed a sense of the worth of the individual, but without an adequate conception of responsibility for society, and therefore, it led to an unduly loose organization of the family. But Christian thought took up the Teuton contribution and has made most helpful use of it.

Without giving additional illustrations, it is enough to say that for nineteen centuries the religion of the Christ has largely, and mainly, been an adapting and adopting power, a leaven leavening human thought and life with the Christian spirit. In general, the principle of evolution has ever been at work. Through the best elements in the thought and life of all peoples there has been a preparation everywhere for the Christ. Under the influence of the Holy Spirit when the dynamic of the Christ had leavened the thought and institutions of any nation, the old religion gradually passed away, but not without having done something for the world. What God has done for and through every other people, He has undoubtedly been doing for the Hindu. As He brings India into contact with the Christ, the Christ will enter into the preparation of the past and will fulfil all of India's best thought and life till every jot and tittle is utilized, and through the Christianized thought and life of India God will enrich the world.

This preliminary statement has made it plain why I do not say that God has prepared India to accept Christianity. Christianity ought to mean only the teaching and the power of the Lord Jesus Christ. But the words Christ and Christianity are not commensurate nor interchangeable. Every thoughtful, sensitive, occidental Christian knows that his own thought and life and institutions and local church are not completely Christlike, and of course that so-called Christianity and churches and peoples of the

West are only partially Christian. Therefore, it is proper, prudent, and reverent to the Lord of our lives not commonly to use the word Christianity in connections which will cause non-Christians to assume that we suppose Christ and Christianity to be entirely interchangeable terms.

If a sense of the inadequacy of any section of the Christian Church's being an incarnation of the Christ is clear to occidentals who bear the Christian name, it is more clear to the oriental who has frequent and disillusionizing experience of contact with unchristian men and proposals which take the Christian name. This cannot be helped. God is most long-suffering toward all who take the Christian name, as toward all who do not. To the occidental the word Christianity practically means his own interpretation of religious thought and life. To the oriental still more does the word Christianity mean the Western interpretation of religion expressed in thought, life, and institution. Partly with good reason and perhaps partly without adequate reason, such interpretation does not wholly appeal to him. But no Christian sees any deficiency in the Lord Jesus Christ, and every Christian man and every Christian Church wishes all men to accept and to follow the Christ. So the wise way is humbly to recognize our limitations, and to say to orientals and to non-Christians everywhere: "Follow the Christ, not me." Or, we may say with Paul: "Follow me so far as I follow the Christ." Therefore, loyalty to Christ will lead us to speak of how God has been preparing India for the Christ, and how Christ is fitted to meet that preparation. We all desire to make the Christ Himself supreme. He said: "I, if I be lifted up, will draw all men unto Me," not to Christianity, not to any particular interpretation of Myself.

Not only so, but we should humbly and gladly live under the encouraging assurance of the evolutionary working of the Holy Spirit, expressed by the writer of the Epistle to the Hebrews, thus: "God having provided some better things concerning us, that apart from us they [i.e. even the prophets and saints of an earlier dispensation] should not be made perfect." On that principle the

Christians of to-day should entertain the inspiring, though humbling, conviction that till all the races of the world pay allegiance to the Christ and make their interpretation of Him, the most favoured of previous Christian communities shall not be perfect. For our present thought that implies that when such peoples as the Hindus accept and interpret the Christ, they will make valuable contributions to the thought and life of God's children everywhere.

As another preliminary consideration bearing on this topic, we might well bear in mind the apostle Paul's word: "A veil lieth upon their heart. But whensoever a man shall turn unto the Lord, the veil shall be taken away." Paul did not think of some religions as false and of one as true. He thought of God as trying to enlighten all men, and of all men as straining to see God, but of most men as having a veil over their spiritual vision which prevents them from adequately seeing God. But when men shall see God as the Man Christ Jesus reveals Him, then the veil will be taken away; and, if men steadily and sincerely behold the glorious revelation of God which is made by Christ, then by the Spirit of God they will gradually be more and more changed into likeness to Him. Now it is an interesting coincidence that to the Hindu all nature and all the experiences of life seem a veil. He sadly recognizes that his view of God is hindered, not helped, by what we consider God's work in nature, in man, and in history. To the Hindu this is all veil, which by prolonged meditation he seeks to pierce and to push away. To him everything in the phenomenal world is unreal, something which hinders his getting close to and united with the Real and Divine. The Christian believes that that veil which seems to the Hindu to obscure his vision of God will be removed whensoever the Hindu shall steadily gaze into the face of the Lord Jesus Christ, the perfect Man, and in that clear mirror the Hindu will, by the Holy Spirit, secure the liberty which will free him from the bondage of the past and of caste; and then, beholding the glory of the Lord, he shall by that Spirit be more and more transformed into the image of the Christ Himself. Not only Paul's, but also Christ's thought is that He did not come to destroy previous religions or to found the Christian religion. We may be thankful that Christ did not speak of a religion or of religions, but of coming to enlarge the kingdom of God, the family of the heavenly Father, to help men to live aright, to have life and that abundantly.

With such preliminary considerations let us now turn to consider how God has been preparing India for the Christ and how the Christ is fitted to meet and to fulfil that preparation. But first I recall the last point of the previous lecture, viz.: that Hinduism as a religion is breaking down because it cannot meet the tests and requirements of modern life. That seems to me incontrovertible. Something must take the place of the old religion, for the Indians are the most religious people in the world. To lose their old religion and not to have a better one take its place would be the experience of having one evil spirit cast out and to have seven worse evil spirits come in. God forbid that such a disaster should ever come to beloved India!

Yet there is a danger. In December, 1882, when a Decennial Conference of Indian missionaries was held in Calcutta, on the evening preceding the Conference, at the solicitation of several missionaries, Keshab Chandar Sen, the leader of the most advanced section of the Brahma Samāj, made an address especially intended for missionaries. He began his address by saying for substance: "Fathers and Brethren, I should never have ventured to take upon myself to speak to a company like you unless some of your own members had pressed it on me that some thoughts might be suggestive and helpful from one who is not of your number, but who reveres your Lord and Master Jesus Christ, and who is grateful for your services to my country." The burden of his address was an appeal something like this: "While the contact of the West with India has done and is doing, my country great good, yet it is also doing one serious injury. Of old India's ideals were spiritual. Our ancestors did not aspire after wealth, or honour, or power, but after knowledge of the Spirit. However, contact with the practical West is changing the ideals and aspirations of young India. Our young men are becoming eager to amass fortunes, to secure honours, to become powerful in politics and society. India is in danger of becoming materialized. Now who is to withstand and correct this evil tendency which is coming to this country from yours, if not you, disciples of the Christ, men of the Spirit? I appeal to you to consider whether, in view of this growing danger, you cannot see your way more and more to concentrate your attention and your efforts on developing spiritual life among our young men. Can you not leave to educated Indians the teaching of secular subjects in schools and colleges, and yourselves expend your strength on spiritual subjects in order to develop spiritual life?"

Unquestionably contact with modern life is surely undermining Hinduism. Something must take its place. The Christian believes and must act as if he believed that the Christ can save India from growing materialism. If so, He must and will do it by fulfilling the best elements of India's thought and life by His own revelation and dynamic. India will be Christianized only as Christian thought and life are naturalized in it.

Even the higher Hinduism cannot meet the tests of the modern spirit, first, because Hinduism assumes the unreality of the world, whereas modern life says that reality is nowhere if it is not always near and in and all about us, that in the highest degree the real is personal, not impersonal, and therefore is ethical and spiritual; secondly, because Hinduism assumes that the attainment of reality is by escaping from the world into practical non-existence, whereas modern life says: "For your own sake and for the world's sake stay *in* the world and do your very best to make the world better;" "'tis life, not death, for which we pant, more life and fuller that we want;" thirdly, the modern spirit requires that no thought, or institution, or influence be contracted or mechanical or even national; that the golden age of nothing shall be deemed to be in the past; that what the human spirit needs must be universal, progressive, spiritual, genuinely human. Also, though the Neo-Hindu may not know or think it, the modern spirit requires that the obligation of the highest is best to serve the lowest, that only by such an attitude and service can the highest remain high and rise still higher. The higher Hinduism cannot meet any of these tests, and therefore must pass away. Yet the man of insight distinctly sees in this very crisis and in India's past history which has led up to this crisis God's preparation of India for the Christ, and Christ's fitness to fulfil India's highest, deepest need.

Now what are some of India's preparations for the Christ? First, India's long and patient thinking has been preparing her for a more balanced, a more personal apprehension of unity in the universe. In no country more than in India has there been patient effort to find a basis for unity. The impersonal monism of the thinkers, though severely logical, has not been satisfactory, because it did not meet all the needs of the whole nature of man. By Indian thinkers religion was sacrificed to, and made identical with, philosophy. No wonder that this has proved insufficient. India needs a thinking which satisfies the intellect, and yet which also satisfies the heart and conscience.

When by her wisdom India sought to know God, yet knew not God, she was being prepared at the fulness of time, through the Christ, who is the wisdom and the power of God, to know the one and only true and personal God whom to know is life eternal. The Christ gives such a satisfying revelation of unity in the universe as fulfils India's longing, and such as India can well interpret to the world. India's craving for a consistent explanation of unity has not been satisfied by the hypothesis of impersonal monism, but it is a preparation for the Christ's revelation that the unity of the universe of sentient beings is a personal monism. Christ did not teach this as a philosophy but as life, because that is the way in which the world needs truth. The way in which He expressed the truth of a personal monism was this: "I and the Father are one." "That they may all be one; even as Thou, Father, art in Me and I in Thee, that they may also be one in Us." . . . "That they may be one, even as we are one; I in them, and Thou in Me, that they may be perfected into one." This unity of personal monism is the vital principle in the most suggestive and mystical of Christ's parables, such as that of the vine and branches, and that of the body and its members.

We may be thankful that Christ did not put this teaching in philosophical form, because until recently the Christian world in the West was not prepared to receive such truth. But contact with India has strengthened the growing demand of thoughtful Christian men in the West to see the necessity for and the helpfulness of personal monism as the satisfactory interpretation of the unity of the universe. According to this thought, man is a real personal being, but not separate from God as an entirely independent existence. He is such a projection of God as a son is a projection of his parents; and because God is a person, the human projection of God must partake of His personal characteristics. Men have intelligence, heart, and will, as God has. The personal qualities of the source must be in those who come out from, and yet are inseparably connected with, that source. And in the vast, mysterious realm of the subliminal or subconscious, which philosophy and psychology are beginning to discover, and the fringes of which they are beginning to explore, we see suggestions of how a personal monism can more satisfactorily than any other hypothesis meet the intellectual demand for unity, and yet can give full play to personality in man. We can see the wisdom of the Christ in speaking of these profound themes in terms of life and not of philosophy. Wisely He ever spoke of the relation of men to God as that of children to a father. Yet is not philosophy suggesting that children and parents are not wholly independent, separated beings? And Paul well used religious language in accord with his doctrine of personal monism, when he said of God: "In Him we live, and move, and have our being." Spiritual-minded men are seeing that the pantheistic trend of Hindu thought was a preparation for the Christ. In the doctrine that the unity of the universe is in a divine personal monism, the deepest things of Christ fulfil the preparation which was in Hindu thought. The Christ was fond of calling Himself "The Light of the World." Light is a help for the mind. Since the Christ is the light of the intellectual world, He is the one to satisfy the unsatisfied, intellectual requirements of the Hindu.

Secondly, for millenniums the Hindu has patiently sought, not only for the ultimate unity of the universe, but for reality. Starting from the misleading hypothesis of impersonal monism, the Hindu could consistently find reality nowhere. Yet he panted after reality, though he never found it. On the Christian explanation of God and the universe that the unity of the universe is that of a personal God in whom all live, and move, and have their being, the demand of the Hindu mind and heart for reality can be satisfied. As light was one great word of Christ, so truth was another. Truth is the touchstone of reality. Christ not only called Himself the truth, but said that He is the way to truth, He is the life of truth. To the Hindu the divine has been the great unknown, unsearchable, unconscious It. The

Christ says, God is a Spirit (i.e. a personal being who has intelligence, heart, and will), Therefore, those who worship Him, must worship Him in spirit (i.e. with thought, with love, and with determination); and thus worshipping intelligently, lovingly, and volitionally must worship God in truth. And the spirit of man can thus worship the divine Spirit because man is a projection of that divine Spirit, who Himself seeks the human spirit. Because they both are of one piece they are mystically and eternally united.

While the Hindu has, for the most part, thought of the ultimate reality as impersonal, yet he has also spoken of It as being *satchidananda,* i.e. as being or having existence, intelligence, and bliss. To the Hindu this conception has been vague. The Christ clarifies this vague Hindu belief by His plain inspiring teaching that God is a Spirit, i.e. in the very highest sense a personal being with heart, mind, and will. With such a conviction as to the nature of God and the nature of man, the Hindu longing for reality is met. Now every man can have absolute confidence in himself as real, and in his mental and spiritual activities as real; whereas, on the Hindu assumption of impersonal monism, man himself and all his activities, and all the phenomena of the universe, were illusory and unreal. Oh Christ, how marvellously Thou wilt help Thy Hindu children into release from *māyā* and unreality, and enable them to walk on solid ground!

The Christ gives His clearest, fullest assurance of the reality of ourselves by showing that He is Himself a man, a full representative man, the Son of Man, and through this revelation of man, He also gives the most satisfactory assurance that God is real, by showing that our final, conclusive test of what God is like and of what God will do, is the action of our own spirits: "What man is there of you, who, if his son shall ask him for a loaf, will he give him a stone? . . . If ye then, being evil, know how to give good gifts unto your children, how much more shall your Father who is in heaven give good things to them that ask Him?" Christ's conviction and teaching of the eternal, absolute dependableness of all sound human activities and conclusions is shown in His constant teaching by parables, the assumption being that God and all men think alike, and act alike, and are reliable. So India's long craving for reality has been a preparation for the truth-giving Christ, who fulfils the Hindu's longing for reality.

Thirdly, while the previous lecture has shown that India longs for largeness, yea, infinity, yet most of her people have longed for, and tried to find, some manifestation of the great unknown which is near, which is visible, which is approachable, which responds to the appeal of human need. This is the psychological explanation of idolatry, of the deification of saints, and of belief in incarnations. Both high and low, philosopher and peasant, saint and sinner, have craved and believed that they had found some helpful incarnation. Yet they themselves have shown that they had not been satisfied because numerous unsatisfactory incarnations have followed one after another. And the clearest evidence of the Hindu's preparation for the Christ is the well-nigh universal anticipation of another incarnation to come, the Kalki Avatar, who is to be both a human and a divine incarnation and one to be stained by suffering.

In theory the Mohammedan stoutly controverts the possibility of any incarnation of the divine in the human. Yet he practically expresses a demand for something like an incarnation by his always coupling the name of the prophet of Mecca with Allah in his oft-repeated call to worship. Also the Mohammedan looks for a coming prophet greater than Mohammed and one who will replace him. God has been preparing both Hindu and Mohammedan for finding in the Christ a perfect manifestation of the divine in, and through, a perfect human being, divine because He is perfect.

Fourthly, the intellect, the conscience, and the heart of India have all been baffled in their search for a solution of the haunting problem of unmerited suffering. They could not rest without some profound, far-reaching explanation. Because no other adequate solution had been shown, India sought in abstract justice, without any consideration of love, the logical basis of an explanation of the mystery of undeserved suffering. The logical explanation by an hypothesis that the mystery of apparently unmerited trouble is in the necessity of retribution in the present life of wrong-doing in a previous unremembered existence was unsatisfying, because it allowed no room for a thought or influence of love. However, love cannot come into consideration when there is no personal God, but only an impersonal It to explain the mystery of the world. Instinctively recognizing the unsatisfactoriness of the Karma doctrine, the Hindu sought Release from it in the allied, but equally unsatisfying, doctrine of transmigration. In the transmigration doctrine, too, there is no thought of love. In all of India's patient, dissatisfied mental search, there is no more pathetic and conclusive evidence of her longing for a more satisfying conclusion than in her thinking that she had found the explanation of the universe in the action of abstract justice, which makes the sole object of the world an opportunity for the retributive requital of past wrong-doing, and then of Release from this system by practical non-existence.

How evidently that longing of the Hindu heart has prepared it for the need of a fulfilment through a revelation of the divine love, and how perfectly the Christ, and only the Christ, can supply the fulfilment!

From the Christ the Christian has learned first, that the unmerited sufferings of the Christ were voluntary and were joyfully endured. Of His own will, for love's sake, at the hands of evil men whom He loved, He bore such sufferings as none other have borne, even to the last extremity on the cross. "For the joy that was set before Him, He endured the cross, despising the shame"; secondly, that the unmerited sufferings of the Christ are a revelation of the heart of God in His tender compassion toward sinful children. "God so loved the world that He gave His only begotten Son, that whosoever believeth in Him should not perish, but have everlasting life"; thirdly, the Christian sees that the result of Christ's undeserved sufferings is the awakening of repentance in sinners, of changing their hearts, of making them loyal to God and ready themselves to suffer for the salvation of erring fellow men.

What the Christ has been doing for other peoples, He is actually now doing for Hindus. When the Christ said: "I, if I be lifted up, will draw *all* men unto me," of course He included the Hindus. From personal knowledge through thirty-six years of service in India, I testify that, on a large scale, the suffering Christ, more than the teaching Christ, is drawing both the ignorant and the learned, both the degraded and refined, marvellously to Himself, and through Himself to God, and into willing suffering for erring fellow men.

Fifthly, in asceticism the Hindu has shown an unsatisfied longing which will lead him to find fulfilment in the Christ, which fulfilment the Christ is fitted to supply. In the belief that the world is unreal, that the object of life is, at any cost, by utmost self-denial to escape from the unreal, the unworthy, into some vague better state, millions of Hindus have for centuries voluntarily and continuously undergone self-denial, deprivation, abnegation, torture, of which men of the West can form no conception. The weakness of the Hindu has not been the Westerner's weakness of satisfaction with material comfort and indifference to the highest ideal, but a conscientious, persistent pursuit of what was deemed the highest good. But through the pursuit of a mistaken ideal, it was a sad waste of the possibilities of full and noble life. As the modern spirit dissolves the Hindu's conception of the world, of men, of God, and of the object of life, and as the old reasons for asceticism lose their lure, for what has this ascetic phase of Hindu thought and life been preparing itself and how will it find fulfilment? Is not India's ascetic past a marvellous preparation for a deep appreciation of the Christ who reveals God as the great sufferer, the One who must deny Himself for the good of His erring children? "God commendeth His love toward us, in that, while we were yet sinners, Christ died for us." Under the inspiration of such an example may we not expect that Christian India will gladly take up its cross and follow Christ in order to help weak and sinning brother men?

Also the Christ reveals and fulfils the true reason for self-sacrifice to be not the ascetic reason of making one's self perfect, but of thereby serving fellow men and pleasing the heavenly Father. "The Son of Man came not to be ministered unto, but to minister and to give His life a ransom for many." Moreover, in the finest book of Hinduism, the Bhagavad Gita, it is taught that the good man is to do good without any desire for reward. But human nature being what it is, that half truth of the value of doing good without desire for reward has no dynamic without the complementary truth which the Christ taught and illustrated, viz.: that one should gladly suffer and serve, in order to please one's heavenly Father, apart from desire for personal gain. Teaching that one should serve in this way, the Christ said: "Love your enemies, . . . that ye may be sons of your Father who is in heaven; . . . if ye love them that love you . . . do not even the publicans the same? . . . Be ye perfect as your heavenly Father is perfect." And the Christ taught how an unsought for, unexpected blessing will come to those who serve Him, in serving their fellow men, when He said: "Then shall the king say,

Come, ye blessed of my Father. *I* was hungry and ye gave me to eat." And when those who had been unselfishly benevolent shall say, with amazement: "When saw we *Thee* hungry and fed *Thee?*" the king shall answer: "Inasmuch as ye did it unto one of these my brethren, even these least, ye did it unto Me."

Sixthly, the Hindu doctrine of the Spirit calls for a fulfilment which only the Christ can give. It seems almost incredible that in a land which, on the surface, seems given over to idolatry, ceremonialism, superstition, much degradation, and grinding poverty, it should be true that the ideal of even the ignorant and poor should be of the Spirit as the great reality. To the educated and philosophical, the Spirit was the *only* reality. The Hindu thinker and the plain man constantly speak of the Spirit, the Atman, and of the Supreme Spirit, the Paramātman. But to them the ultimate reality being an impersonal monism, they could not apply to that Supreme Spirit an adjective of moral meaning. Nor did even the Hebrew prophets do much of this. In the Old Testament there are limited references to the Spirit of God, but not the expression, the Holy Spirit. The chief gift of the Christ to the Christian has been His teaching about the Holy Spirit just before His own departure from the world, and His imparting of the Holy Spirit after the resurrection. As to the Christian, the Holy Spirit is the fulfilment and the fulfiller of even the deepest things of Christ, so to the Hindu, with his recognition of the Spirit as the supreme reality, there will come only through the Christ a fulfilment of the conception of the Spirit as holy.

Without attempting to specify other points in which India has been prepared for a fulfilment of thought and life by the Christ and of the Christ's fitness to supply that fulfilment, I mention in conclusion the supreme Hindu institution of caste. As indicated in the third lecture, the institution of caste started with proper natural reasons, and its basal assumption is that of the unitedness of men as actual members one of another with reciprocal serviceableness and duties. But falling from that natural proper starting point, it has largely become an unbrotherly, unprogressive, tyrannical institution, injurious to society and to religion. However, since the Christ came not to destroy, but to fulfil institutions, as well as beliefs, and since He will not let one jot or one tittle of law or institution pass away without being fulfilled, it is inspiring to think of how India needs a fulfilment of her characteristic institution, which, though debased, calls for fulfilment, and to anticipate how the Christ is fitted to save to the uttermost, not only individuals, but also institutions.

Even the Christian West is only beginning to recognize that society is an inseparable, indissoluble organism of which God is the head, the life, the source, and therefore, that the smallest member of society is actually connected with God and with every other human being. It has taken nineteen centuries for the Western church and Western civilization to begin adequately to understand this fundamental truth. When the conception of a personal monism is the philosophical basis for an adequate interpretation of the universe of sentient beings, and when a growing appreciation of the vast, mysterious subliminal life shows how every man is a personal projection from the personal God, ever actually in connection with Him, and therefore, with every other human being, society will more adequately appreciate the value of the basal truth in the caste system, and will marvel that India first developed that formative principle on a large scale.

But under the downward pull of the flesh that idea of society got twisted in India in at least two ways. First, instead of seeing that privilege brought responsibility, the upper caste reversed the order and imagined that society is, and should be, ordered so that the lower shall exist for, and serve the upper, and that the relations and conditions which have once been formed should be stationary and hereditary. Second, caste limited the unitedness of men to those within the Hindu pale. Therefore, at present, Hindu society has nothing to give to others, and nothing to receive from them. A non-Hindu could never become a Hindu, and the golden age of Hinduism being in its past, it could get nothing from others. It was a most heinous sin for a Hindu to leave India to go to other countries, even in the desire to benefit his native land. To-day no one thing is more evident in India than a sense of injury from caste as it exists.

However, the basal system of caste was not wrong. A social institution which recognizes, as no other system has done, the unitedness and community of interest of every member of a group has elements of great value which need to be conserved and fulfilled. Only the Christ can do this. He teaches as no one ever did that *every* human being is a child of the heavenly Father, most dear to that Father, and therefore a brother of every other human being, and therefore every one who would be true to his heavenly Father must be loving to every brother man; that if one member suffers, all suffer; that we who are strong ought to bear the infirmities of the weak, and not to please ourselves; that if a man loves not his brother whom he hath seen, he cannot love God whom he has not seen. Thus the Christ removes, not only the first mischievous

Hindu subversion, and fulfils the correct basal principle of caste that all Hindus are indissolubly connected with one another in order that the higher may serve the lower, but Christ also removes the second subversion which limits the unitedness of men to those who are within the Hindu pale, and fulfils it by showing that all men of every race are brethren. By life He shows this through leading Christians from distant lands to manifest that they have brotherly feelings by their going to India to serve brother men there.

I am not only making a forecast of what Christ *could* do to fulfil the elements of India's past thought and life, but I can show that He actually *is* thus fulfilling that preparation. The Christ is not only the wisdom of God, but still more is He the power of God. First, every one who knows India intimately knows that while the most spiritual men of that country are not being numerously drawn to identify themselves with the Christian Church, and while some object to the creeds and institution of the Western organization of Christianity, they are increasingly and generally being drawn to a reverence for the Christ and for spiritual discipleship to Him.

Many concrete illustrations could be given. Time permits of only one. On the fourteenth of June, 1910, at the Central Y.M.C.A. Hall in Bombay, the Vice-Chancellor of the University of Bombay, who is a Justice of the Bombay High Court, a Hindu gentleman of the highest standing, who does not call himself a Christian, made an address on "The Kingdom of Christ and the Spirit of the Age." Among other things, he said: "I should like to say at the outset that it is not an easy thing for me to stand on this platform and address a Christian audience on the Kingdom of Christ and the Spirit of the Age. Let me tell you what I consider the greatest miracle of the present day; it is this: that to this great country with its three hundred millions of people, there should come from a little island unknown by name even to our forefathers, many thousand miles distant from our shores, and with a population of but fifty to sixty millions, a message so full of spiritual life and strength as the Gospel of Christ. This surely is a miracle, if ever there was one. And this message has not only come, but it is finding a response in our hearts, for as I have already indicated to you, the old conception of a spiritual worship of God has not entirely perished from the minds of the people, though it may be buried below a mass of ceremony and superstition. The process of the conversion of India to Christ may not be going on as rapidly as you hope, or in exactly the manner that you hope, but, nevertheless, I say India is being converted; the ideas that lie at the heart of the Gospel of Christ are slowly, but surely, permeating every part of Hindu society and modifying every phase of Hindu thought. And this process must go on so long as those who preach this Gospel seek, above all things, to commend it, not so much by what they say, but by what they do and the way they live. And what is it in the Gospel of Christ that commends it so highly to our minds? It is just this: that He was 'the friend of sinners'; He would eat and drink with publicans and outcasts; He was tender with the woman taken in sin; all His heart went out to the sinful and needy; and to my mind there is no story so touching and so comforting as the Prodigal Son. Christ reserved His words of sternest denunciation for hypocrites, and especially for religious hypocrites whose lives and conduct utterly belie the great professions that they make. The Gospel of the Kingdom of Christ has come to India, and when it is presented in its fulness and lived in its purity, it will find a sure response among the people of the land. . . . I have no right to speak at all about the Kingdom of Christ; but I believe that it is working amongst us to-day; it is the little leaven that will in time leaven the entire mass. The Kingdom of Christ, I say, is working out its own ends, slowly, silently, and yet securely."

In the West, God has led Christians in ways which, on the whole, have commended the Christ to their minds and hearts. They have made mistakes. The flesh has sometimes conquered the spirit. But protests and reforms have been made, and increasingly the West has come to obey the guidance of the Holy Spirit, to interpret the Christ better, and to serve brother men more gladly and effectively. The creeds, the institutions, the modes of worship, and of organization have, on the whole, proved helpful. We should revere the past, and therefore these origins of our religious faith and life. Some of them are proving somewhat helpful to the thought and life of non-Christian brother men in other lands. They may prove still more helpful.

However, certainly in India and Japan, and somewhat in China, these Western interpretations are proving to many not attractive, but rather repellent. Yet multitudes in those countries are being vitally drawn to the Christ. We may well have such absolute confidence in the Holy Spirit that we shall trust Him to guide India as He has guided the people of every other land, into that interpretation and discipleship of the Christ into which He shall guide them. But the one thing which all history and genetic psychology and the evolutionary doctrine unquestionably teach is that India's Christianization should be, and will be, in the development of her past history under the tutelage of the Holy Spirit, unfolding and applying the principles of Him who is the Son of Man and the Son of God, the Lord Jesus Christ. Under the dynamic of the Christ and under the guidance of the Holy Spirit, the future religion of India will be one which is "a full re-expression of the religious spirit" of all sections of that very religious people. Christian thought and life must, and will be, domesticated in India before they become general there.

Western Christians have a great responsibility and a great privilege in helping India to know and appreciate the Christ. But in the main, they must be, and will be, like John the Baptist, a voice making ready the way of the Christ. Like John they must think and say of the Christ: "His shoes we are not worthy to bear; He shall baptize you with the Holy Spirit and in fire." "We must decrease and He must increase." Like the great apostle we should think and say: "Christ sent us not to baptize, but to preach the Gospel." While Western Christians have their creeds, and while most of them require subscription to elaborate creeds, it is suggestive that none of them give a brief, all-sufficient creed entirely in New Testament language. It is also a suggestive fact that Hinduism never had and now has not one simple creed nor several credal statements, which can be deemed authoritative. The spiritual Indian, who comes into discipleship to the Christ and who makes the Holy Spirit his perpetual divine teacher and guide, is not likely to think subscription to Western creeds of the past essential to his taking the Christ as Lord and Master. He will take the Holy Spirit as spiritual guide and strengthener. But India is *sure* to be a disciple of the Christ.

> "Oh, Christ is Christ, and rest is rest,
> And love true love must greet.
> In East and West hearts crave for rest;
> And so the twain shall meet;
> —The East still East and the West still West,—
> At Love's nail-piercèd feet."

And the Kingdom of God shall have come.

INDEX